GW00786717

THE ST
CANTERBURY C......
150 YEARS 1842-1992

by
Christopher H. Taylor
Foreword by E. W. Swanton

This book is dedicated to The Kent County Cricket Club for the many years of pleasure and enjoyment it has provided me and to my wife (Joan) for her tolerance and understanding.

Designed and printed by Geerings of Ashford Limited.

The Story of Canterbury Cricket Week –
1842-1992

Preface

A S a devotee of Kent cricket for more years than I care to recall
I have a special affection for Canterbury's St Lawrence ground
and its grand festival week. No matter the weather, dull or bright,
the first sight of the ground on that opening day stirs up in me
memories of bygone times and a sense of great pride in being
present and part of the oldest and most historical of Cricket Weeks.

Many that attend today are unaware of the great history of the
'Week', something that cannot be matched. In this book I hope to
enlighten those too young to remember this great story so that
they will more readily understand what it all means: to tell the tale
of those such as the Old Stagers, I. Zingari, and the Band of
Brothers and the parts they have played in building the great
traditions of the 'Week', for they, as much as the cricket, have
played a very important part in its story.

I would like to thank Mr. E. W. Swanton, my fellow curator, for
all the help and encouragement he has given me in the writing of
this book. Without that help and encouragement I fear it would not
have been completed. I would also like to thank him for writing a
foreword.

Introduction

'CANTERBURY Cricket Week': three words that conjure up in the minds of cricket lovers throughout the world a picture of numerous multi-coloured tents in a semi-circle, each identified by the flags flying above them, that partially encircle the St Lawrence ground in early August each year: military bands, in scarlet uniforms, playing for the entertainment of visitors and members during intervals in play: Ladies Day, when the scene is enhanced by the spectacle of lady guests promenading around the ground in bright summer dresses and hats for all to admire, to the strains of majestic military music: but perhaps not least, the famous lime tree that stands gloriously in full leaf within the field of play, as it has done throughout the history of the 'Week'.

Conceived in 1841 and born in 1842, the 'Week' celebrates its 150th anniversary in 1992. This is not intended to be a year by year narrative of matches and events during the Century and a half so much as the story of its formative years: the early battles between Kent and England and its progress to modern days. It will also relate some of the exciting finishes to matches and just a few of the deeds of some of the great players and personalities who have appeared in the 'Week'. Over such a long period it was inevitable that changes would take place, the outbreak of two world wars being a major feature leading to the changes in social habits. With the growth of the public transport system and, later, the coming of the motor car, it became much easier to travel to and from the ground each day, avoiding the need to stay within the city.

The main ingredients of the 'Week', fine cricket in a spectacular setting, exciting finishes and players performing worthy deeds for their sides, have all survived the passing of time. But the 'Week' is not only about the cricket. There is the social side and the theatre presentations each evening throughout the week by the Old Stagers, whose story is told in another chapter as are those of 'I Zingari' and the Band of Brothers, each of whom have a very close association with the 'Week' and have played a very important role in ensuring the popularity and success it has enjoyed and maintained. We can only wonder what the fate of this, the most historical and oldest of cricket weeks, would be if the Championship were to consist only of 4-day matches. We can only hope that it would survive this change, if it happens, as it has all the others and that it will go to its 200th and beyond for future generations to enjoy as we have done.

KENT CLUB,

1842.

GRAND

Cricket Match

KENT *against* ENGLAND,

ON THE

Beverley Ground,

Adjoining the Cavalry Barracks, Canterbury,

ON

MONDAY, August 1, 1842,

And following Days.

PLAYERS.

KENT.	ENGLAND.
W. de C. BAKER, Esq.	Hon. F. PONSONBY
F. FAGGE, Esq.	G. LANGDON, Esq.
N. FELIX, Esq.	C. G. TAYLOR, Esq.
A. MYNN, Esq.	BARKER
W. MYNN, Esq.	BOX
C. G. WHITAKER, Esq.	FENNER
ADAMS	GOOD
DORRINTON	GUY
HILLIER	HAWKINS
MARTINGALE	LILLYWHITE
PILCH	REDGATE
WENMAN	SEWELL

UMPIRES—MILLS and BAYLEY.

The MILITARY BAND will be in attendance.

An original handbill advertising the first Canterbury Cricket Week 1842.

5

Foreword

by E. W. Swanton

I T is a pleasure, writing close on the conclusion of the 150th Canterbury Week, to give a brief send-off to the painstaking work of my fellow-Curator, Christopher Taylor. It would have been sad if this milestone in Kentish history had been cool and wet, as even August days can be. As it is, our recollection of the 1991 edition will be of much admirable cricket in the loveliest sunny weather and amid the graceful trappings of tents and bands and bunting which make this annual celebration a thing apart. What was equally fitting was that Kent had moral victories over both Surrey and Hampshire. It was a feat to make Surrey follow on twice in the season – at the Oval they had been beaten by an innings. The Hampshire match would probably have been won but for the Stygian gloom which meant the loss of half the play after tea on the 2nd day – the only temporary break in the weather all week.

Those of us who have been lucky enough to attend many Canterburys may have certain recollections pickled, as it were, in the mind. With the utmost clarity I can see three. The first, not surprisingly, surrounds the great Frank Woolley. Nottinghamshire were the visitors, and there had been enough rain to make the ball fly. Frank, tall, majestic, came in first as he liked to do in his latter years because he said he could see the new ball better than the old, and the Notts fast bowlers made the cardinal mistake of pitching short to him. They found themselves cut and hooked with withering power, the bat from that high back-lift coming down on the ball with an echoing crack. Frank was 47 at the time and his hundred arrived soon after one o'clock, just a shade more slowly than his first, made at Tonbridge in an hour and a half just 28 years before. What a hero to cherish through life!

Just before the war, Notts came again to the Week, and Bryan Valentine's generous declaration was made to look like a present by Joe Hardstaff, tall and fair, a proper deb's delight, whose driving, likewise from a high back-lift and with the hands at the top of his long-handled Gunn and Moore bat, brought him a hundred in 51 minutes. It was the fastest of the summer and the fastest I ever saw.

6

My third picture is more personal in that I was involved to the extent of being on the air at the moment when Leslie Ames reached his hundredth hundred and so able to tell the world via the old BBC Home and Overseas Services. His innings, as always, was shaped to the needs of the occasion and it enabled Kent to win a race against the clock. Middlesex were the opponents, 1950 the year, and he came dancing down the pitch to the spinners like a 2-year-old. Yet it proved my old friend's last hundred for Kent, for early the following season his back "went" and he could play no more. What services he went on to render to both England and Kent cricket is, of course, inscribed in history.

C ANTERBURY Week, of course, as Christopher Taylor relates in this nostalgic, fondly-written book, was an event long before the County Championship was thought of. Even after the formation of the County Club in 1870 there was no immediate concentration on Canterbury. In 1875 Kent played all their home county matches at Catford Bridge, in a setting far removed from St. Lawrence. That was the significant year wherein — to its great advantage — Lord Harris virtually took over Kent cricket, being simultaneously Captain, President and Honorary Secretary. Soon afterwards County caps were introduced. One had to play in Canterbury Week to be awarded a cap, dark blue in colour as now, and on which Lady Harris embroidered the white horse. The county club purchased the St. Lawrence Ground in 1896. Thereupon permanent buildings began to supplement the tents, notably, of course, the pavilion built in 1900. Simultaneously the Tonbridge Nursery was founded at Tonbridge under Captain William McCanlis, a gifted coach who produced a stream of talented young professionals to add the essential stiffening to the distinguished but peripatetic amateur element.

Kent cricket was now truly on the march, with Canterbury Week its natural focus, combining the cricket and social side in its inimitable way. When Kent in 1906 won the first of their four pre-First War Championships they celebrated the Week with victories by an innings and plenty over Sussex and Lancashire. The latter match was, of course, the occasion of our great picture by Chavallier Tayler showing Colin Blythe bowling to J. T. Tyldesley. With all their stars available Kent in those days were almost unbeatable in Canterbury Week. So it almost was in the inter-war years. When August came round the county more often than not were still in the Championship with a chance. That was the heyday of Ames and Freeman and Chapman and Valentine and other heroes fit to march in the august shadow of the one and only Frank.

Bryan Valentine, most-characteristic of cricketers and captains, marked the first match of the first post-war Week with a hundred, as also did that talented though enigmatic character Leslie Todd as Hampshire were beaten by an innings. But though the Week continued to hold its charms and three great Kent cricketers, Doug Wright, Godfrey Evans and then Colin Cowdrey held the stage for England, the county's recovery was slow. 1964 however was a turning-point for the better, Cowdrey marking it in the Week in his best style with innings of 99, 100 not out, 101 and 40.

The county's years of glory, wherein 11 titles were won between 1967 and 1978, were reflected in the Weeks of those years wherein a splendid generation re-found much of the attraction of an earlier age. This was the era of yesterday wherein Alan Knott and Derek Underwood made their fame and Mike Denness and Brian Luckhurst formed the most productive opening partnership Kent ever had. Who will forget, too, the oriental magic of Asif Iqbal?

Captains and players come and go: the reigns of Christopher Tavaré and Christopher Cowdrey have been followed by that of Mark Benson, auspiciously begun. There are stresses and strains in the modern game rather different from those which earlier Kent XIs knew. Yet there is a spirit still about Kent cricket, which is nowhere more cherished than in the annual celebration of Canterbury Week.

Sandwich
August 1991

CHAPTER 1

The Story of the Week

FOR a very long time Canterbury has been looked upon as one of the great homes of cricket. In fact Kent had been a force in the game for a hundred years or more before first-class cricket, as we know it today, was played there. A painting, a copy of which hangs in the Chiesman pavilion at Canterbury, shows a game in progress at Petham, on the outskirts of the city, around 1760, whilst between 1773 and 1789 many important matches were played in Bourne Park at Bishopsbourne, the seat of Sir Horace Mann, two or three miles from Canterbury toward Dover. However, on only one occasion before 1841 do records exist of the County playing in Canterbury itself, which was when they played Maidstone on the Old Park in 1777.

Looking back to the earliest records of cricket in Canterbury we find that in 1835, when cricketers played in tall beaver hats, John Baker and William de Chair Baker assisted in forming the Beverley Cricket Club and this is reckoned to be the real beginning of serious cricket in Canterbury.

Where it all began in 1842. The Beverley and East Kent ground Kent v All England.

The Beverley ground was a field behind the house of John Baker on the far side of the now defunct Canterbury/Whitstable railway at St Stephens'. The club's big matches were against the Chilston club and, by 1839, a number of leading players, including Nicholas Felix for Beverley and Alfred Mynn for Chilston, were appearing in these matches. The match in 1839 attracted between three and four thousand spectators, many of them elegantly dressed ladies.

In 1840 the Beverley club moved to a new ground, near the Cavalry barracks in Sturry Road, and renamed it 'The East Kent Cricket Ground', where they were to remain until 1846. In July 1840 Beverley once again played the Chilston club and, for what appears to be the first time, a charge was made for admission to the ground. Over the first two days about 3500 spectators attended and the band of the 13th Dragoons, who were stationed in Canterbury, played on each day of the match. The success of that match, and the interest it aroused, led to Kent playing England on the Beverley ground in 1841. Once again the match attracted a large attendance including many of the county's leading families. It was during this match that a decision was taken to hold a cricket 'Week' in 1842.

The 'Week' was well advertised with arrangements made to welcome a large number of visitors. Theatre performances and a Grand Ball were organised for the evenings and it at once took on the features which have made it quite unlike any other cricket week and certainly one that has never been imitated with any success.

On Monday 1st August 1842 the arrangements for devoting a 'Week' to cricket in Canterbury had been perfected. The amateur actors were prepared to do the portion of duty devolving upon them and the cricketers were no less ready to do theirs. Here is what the 'Kentish Gazette' wrote of the opening day:
"The Beverley ground at eleven o'clock was made the rendezvous of citizens and visitors. The ground was very tastefully laid out. The pavilion, in which a first rate cold collation was spread, and the good things in this life supplied at a liberal charge and of superior quality, under the superintendace of the assiduous host of the Globe Tavern, occupied the farther part of the field and, on each side, in the form of a semi-circle, were marquees, tents, benches and accommodation of all kinds for the spectators. Several of the tents were tastefully ornamented with bouquets of flowers and evergreens which, contrasted with the verdant lawn and the varied coloured dresses of the ladies, produced a very animated and

picturesque scene. There were a considerable number of vehicles upon the ground and we have infinite satisfaction in auguring from this, the first day's display, that the 'Week' will be one of the greatest interest, gaiety and festivity . . . The remainder of the week, if the weather continues favourably, will draw a greater number of visitors to the city than has been known for many years past".

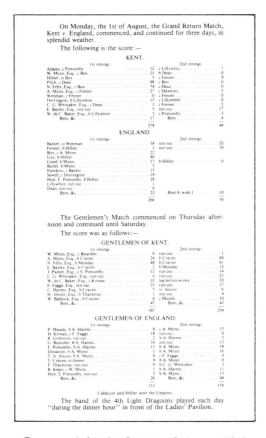

On Monday, the 1st of August, the Grand Return Match, Kent v. England, commenced, and continued for three days, in splendid weather.

The following is the score:—

KENT.

	1st innings		2nd innings	
Adams, c Ponsonby	12	c Lillywhite	7
W. Mynn, Esq., c Box	21	b Dean	0
Hillier, st Box	3	c Fenner	8
Pilch, c Dean	98	c Box	0
N. Felix, Esq., c Box	74	c Dean	0
A. Mynn, Esq., c Fenner	27	c Hawkins	3
Wenman, c Fenner	0	c Fenner	0
Dorrington, b Lillywhite	15	c Lillywhite	0
C. G. Whittaker, Esq., c Dean	3	c Fenner	2
E. Bayley, Esq., not out	5	not out	17
W. de C. Baker, Esq., b Lillywhite	3	c Ponsonby	3
Byes, &c	17	Byes	4
	278		44

ENGLAND.

	1st innings		2nd innings	
Barker, st Wenman	58	not out	20
Fenner, b Hillier	1	not out	19
Box, c A. Mynn	22		
Guy, b Hillier	80		
Good, b Mynn	17	b Hillier	0
Butler, b Mynn	5		
Hawkins, c Barker	15		
Sewell, c Dorrington	19		
Hon. F. Ponsonby, b Hillier	26		
Lillywhite, run out	1		
Dean, not out	0		
Byes, &c.	22	Byes 9, wide 1	10
	266		58

The Gentlemen's Match commenced on Thursday afternoon and continued until Saturday.

The score was as follows:—

GENTLEMEN OF KENT.

	1st innings		2nd innings	
W. Mynn, Esq., c Bourdier	9	run out	1
A. Mynn, Esq., b Craven	24	b Craven	89
N. Felix, Esq., b Munday	48	b Craven	61
E. Bayley, Esq., b Craven	2	b Munday	12
J. Parker, Esq., c S. Ponsonby	12	run out	14
C. G. Whittaker, Esq., run out	0	run out	23
W. de C. Baker, Esq., c Kirwan	10	leg before wicket	20
F. Fagge, Esq., run out	21	run out	17
C. Harenc, Esq., b Craven	5	st. Anson	6
H. Jenner, Esq., b Thackeray	1	not out	9
W. Baldock, Esq., b Craven	6	c Mundy	10
Byes, &c	47	Byes, &c	42
	185		254

GENTLEMEN OF ENGLAND.

	1st innings		2nd innings	
P. Mundy, b A. Harenc	8	c A. Mynn	13
H. Kirwan, c F. Fagge	18	run out	8
R. Grimston, run out	2	b A. Harenc	5
G. Bourdier, b A. Harenc	16	not out	13
F. Ponsonby, b A. Harenc	11	b A. Mynn	19
Dynaston, b A. Mynn	1	b A. Mynn	16
T. A. Anson, b A. Mynn	8	c F. Fagge	9
T. Craven, st Jenner	9	b A. Mynn	0
F. Thackeray, run out	9	b C. G. Whittaker	3
R. Keate, c W. Mynn	1	b A. Harenc	11
Hon. S. Ponsonby, not out	3	b A. Mynn	13
Byes, &c	26	Byes, &c.	44
	112		154

Caldecott and Hillier were the Umpires.

The band of the 4th Light Dragoons played each day "during the dinner hour" in front of the Ladies' Pavilion.

The scorecard of the first Canterbury Cricket week 1842.

H. Hillyer

A. Mynn

Felix

F. Pilch

G. Wenman

With five such mighty cricketers 'twas but natural to win, with Felix, Wenman, Hillyer, Fuller Pilch and Alfred Mynn.

The first match was, as has been said, Kent, with Adams, Walter Mynn, Hillyer, Fuller Pilch, Nicholas Felix, Alfred Mynn, Wenman, Dorrington, C. G. Whittaker, E. Bayley and W. de Chair Baker, against England. The cricket proved worthy of the occasion. Kent made 278 in their first innings, mainly due to two of the greatest batsmen of the day, Fuller Pilch (98) and Nicholas Felix (74). England replied with 266 and, with the wicket badly cut up, Kent were dismissed by Lillywhite and Dean, both of Sussex, for only 44 in their second innings, losing the match by 9 wickets. Typical of one aspect of the cricket in those days the Kent side were commonly believed (without, as far as is known, any justification) to have sold the match and Alfred Mynn was actually hissed in Maidstone market. A wonderful description of the match was given by Fuller Pilch. "Mr Felix, Alfred Mynn and I were in pretty nearly a whole day against eight bowlers and over 750 balls (187.5 four ball overs) bowled in the first hands (innings). Tom Baker and Joseph Guy made the long hands for England and our side bowled as many balls. Kent got 278 and England 266 and then the ground was so cut up that Lillywhite and Dean, without change, got the lot for us for 44 in our second hands and Kent lost by nine wickets."

The second match of this first Canterbury Cricket Week was between the Gentlemen of Kent and the Gentlemen of England which commenced on Thursday afternoon and concluded on Saturday with the Gentlemen of Kent winning by 173 runs. The band of the 4th Light Dragoons played each day, during the dinner hour, in front of the ladies pavilion. The performances at the theatre were of a very superior character. Reports of the day have it that 'many of the amateurs walked the stage with the grace and style of favourite professionals to whom they would have well borne comparison'.

For the first thirteen years of the 'Week' the matches remained the same; in the first half Kent played England and in the second the Gentlemen of Kent opposed the Gentlemen of England. Those were the days when the side were affectionately spoken of as 'the good old Kent eleven' when:

"With five such mighty cricketers 'twas but natural to win,
    As Felix, Wenman, Hillyer, Fuller Pilch and Alfred Mynn."
Of the 31 matches with England between 1835 and 1849, Kent won 17 and lost 13, five of the wins being achieved during the

'Week', two on the Beverley ground (1842 and 1846) and three on the St Lawrence ground.

However, by 1846, some of the older players were past their best and there were no younger players, with the same ability, coming through. Consequently the county's fortunes fell to a low from which they were not to recover for many years and, as a result, England won eight of the next ten matches, two being drawn. When, in 1854, an attempt was made to rectify the situation, Kent used four of England's leading players of the day – John Buckley, William Clark and George Parr of Notts with John Wisden of Sussex – as 'given men'. It was a move that caused much dismay among the county's following. However, it was not a success, for England claimed yet another resounding victory.

For the 1855 fixture Kent combined with Surrey, a combination that brought them victory by 9 runs, but in the second match the combined Gentlemen of Kent and Surrey were not strong enough to defeat the Gentlemen of England. In the hope that the success of 1855 could be repeated both Kent and the Gentlemen of Kent, combined with Sussex in 1856 with the desired result being achieved. For only the second time since 1842, but the first time on the St Lawrence ground, the home side won both matches in the 'Week'. Sadly however, the success could not be repeated in 1857.

Kent again had the assistance of 'given men' – William Caffyn of Surrey and George Parr and John Jackson of Notts – for the match against England in 1858. Jackson took 13 of the 15 England wickets that fell but the Kentish batsmen were unable to maintain the advantage and England won a low scoring match in two days. However, in those days every attempt was made to provide cricket every day so, on the otherwise blank day, I Zingari – of whom we shall read more later – played a drawn one day match with the Gentlemen of Kent. Although matches had finished early on several occasions previously this was only the second time that a full day's play had to be provided. For their match with the Gentlemen of England this year the Gentlemen of Kent were, for the first time, allowed the service of two professionals.

There was no Kent v England match in 1859, instead the North played the South in the first match whilst the Gentlemen of Kent continued their fixture against the Gentlemen of England in the second, the Gentlemen of Kent once again being assisted by two professionals. Kent v England matches were resumed in 1860, and continued until 1864, with Kent fielding sides varying between 13 and 16. Even so success was not always achieved. During this period also the M.C.C. replaced the Gentlemen of England in the second match of the 'Week' but they proved to be just as difficult to beat.

From 1865 to 1873 the first matches of the 'Week' were again North v South, at times billed as North of Thames v South of the Thames, whilst in the second half Kent played the M.C.C. There then followed three years, 1874/76, when Kent combined with Gloucestershire to meet England while the second match was between Kent and M.C.C.

The county side appeared in both matches of the 'Week' in the years 1877-1881 when they again played England and M.C.C. However, 1877 was the last occasion that Kent were to meet England on even terms. Even with W. G. Grace of Gloucestershire and A. W. Ridley of Oxford University and Middlesex in their side as 'given men' in 1877 they could not achieve victory although they did have the better of a draw. For the next four years Kent again fielded sides of 13 to meet England with honours even.

A major change in the fixtures of the 'Week' was brought about in 1882 for, from this date, the matches have always involved Kent and another first-class county, the M.C.C. or the Australians. Kent did not meet the first two Australian touring teams of 1878 and 1880 but between 1882 and 1899 they were to meet on eight occasions when the matches were one of the fixtures of the 'Week'. The period was not a particularly prosperous one in the history of the county club yet five matches were won and three lost.

The 1882 Australians were said to be, at that time, one of the strongest sides to visit these shores, so it was no surprise that they won by seven wickets, despite a fine hundred from E. F. S. Tylecote and fifty in each innings from Mr (later the Rev) C. Wilson, who sometime later became the Bishop of Melanesia. The prestige which the 1884 Australians had gained (they were still a strong side) saw a large number of spectators for the bank holiday fixture.

The match ended after only one and a half hour's play on the third day with a victory for Kent. Amid scenes of great enthusiasm the spectators rushed on to the field and cheered the players and Lord Harris was 'chaired' round the ground.

LORD HARRIS. He did more for Kent cricket than any other man. He captained the side for 15 years between 1875 and 1899.

Kent were to gain a more convincing win in 1886, a victory attributed to the bowling of J. Wootton and the all-round performance of George Hearne. Turner and Ferris were the undoing of many sides when the 1888 Australians toured and Kent were no exception, losing a low scoring match by 81 runs. Good bowling by Walter Wright and Fred Martin supported by an innings of 117 not out from L. A. H. Hamilton in 1890 saw Kent to another victory, Arthur Daffen finishing the match in a blaze of glory by taking four Australian wickets for only five runs. Kent repeated their victory in 1893. Forced to follow-on 102 runs behind, they eventually left the Australians to get 97 for victory but fine bowling by Alec Hearne and Walter Wright saw them put out for 60.

Only three scores of 100 were made against the 1896 Australians one of which was 101 by C. J. Burnup but it was not enough to save Kent from defeat by 176 runs. By contrast the finish to the 1899 match was very exciting. Kent, requiring 138 to win, lost their eighth wicket at 114 but H. C. Stewart and G. J. V. Weigall scored the remaining runs without further loss. The bowling of W. M. Bradley and C. J. Burnup had made the victory bid possible. Sadly however, it was to be the last occasion that the touring team took part in the 'Week'.

The Jubilee meeting 1891.

The scorecard of the Jubilee 'Week'.

From 1900 both matches in the 'Week' have been played against other first-class counties with the exception of 1919 when the Australian Imperial Forces Team took part in the second match of the 'Week'. However, Middlesex (1882), Yorkshire (1885), Lancashire (1888), Gloucestershire (1889), Surrey (1890), Nottinghamshire (1892) and Warwickshire (1892), among the leading first-class counties, had already made their debuts in the 'Week'. Even now, the custom of commencing the 'Week' on a Monday still prevailed. When first-class cricket was resumed after the first world war in 1919, matches were restricted to two days as an experiment but it was a complete failure and in 1920 they reverted to three days. It was from this year too that the present custom of starting on a Saturday was adopted.

Stories concerning matches in the 'Week' are abundant, far too many to relate here in detail. However, one or two are worthy of recalling. On the morning of Monday 11th August 1862, the first day of the 'Week' this year, Hayward of Surrey, was taken ill and unable to play for England with the result that a substitute had to be found. Dr H. M. Grace was on the ground and suggested to Sir Spencer Ponsonby-Fane that he should at once send for his son, E. M. Grace who, at that time was in Bristol. E. M. arrived the next day and scored O and 56. Dr Grace then asked Sir Spencer if E. M. could play for M.C.C. in the second match of the 'Week' but, as E. M. was not then a member of M.C.C. permission was refused. However, when Sir Spencer heard that a member of the M.C.C. team could not make it to Canterbury, he asked William de Chair Baker, the manager of the 'Week', if he would allow E. M. Grace to play. de Chair Baker agreed without consulting W. South Norton, the Kent Captain, who only learned of the arrangement as the match was about to start. The Kent captain protested saying there were other competent cricketers, members of M.C.C., on the ground and he had the support of the whole team when he refused to play the match. An attempt was made to call a meeting of all M.C.C. members present to elect E. M. on the spot, but this was ruled out as being highly irregular.

The Kent team eventually broke the deadlock by agreeing to play on the grounds that the club would suffer serious loss if the spectators had to be given their money back. Imagine then how they must have felt when E. M., after taking five wickets in the first innings of Kent, opened for M.C.C. and carried his bat for 192, the highest individual score recorded on the St Lawrence ground up to that date. He was however, not yet finished for, in the second innings of Kent, he took 10 of the wickets that fell (it was a twelve-a-side match) for 69 runs ensuring his side of victory by an innings and 104 runs. One of the umpires was the celebrated former Kent player Fuller Pilch and there is a story that, early in his innings, E. M. was out to an obvious catch at the wicket but Pilch would not uphold it as he 'wanted to see the young gentleman bat'. The story was never proved.

Another of the Grace brothers, this time the great W. G. himself, must now be the centre of attraction. He first played at Canterbury in 1866 but illness prevented his appearing in 1867. For many years the 'Week' was considered incomplete without his presence. Although he nearly always did well two of his performances made history. In 1868, playing for South against the North, he made 130 in the first innings and 102 not out in the second, the first time the feat of scoring 100 in each innings of a match had been accomplished on the St Lawrence ground and indeed during matches in the 'Week'. Then in 1876 W. G. excelled himself. Against the Gentlemen of M.C.C. Kent had made the then very high score of 473, Lord Harris 154. On Friday, the second day, M.C.C. were bowled out for 144 and, by 5 pm, were forced to follow-on. It appeared to be a hopeless position and W. G., who was due to play at Bristol on the following Monday, anticipated a quiet journey on Saturday with a rest on Sunday. With this in mind he went in to hit and when stumps were drawn at 6.45 the score stood at 217/4, W. G. 133 not out. The following day was very hot but he continued his innings until just before the close when he was out for 344 without having given the semblence of a chance after six hours and twenty minutes batting. His score at that time was the highest individual score recorded in first-class cricket and remains not only the highest of his 126 first-class hundreds but the highest score recorded on the St Lawrence ground to this day. When stumps were finally drawn M.C.C. had taken their score to 557/9. The Kent side were extremely tired and weary with the exception of C. A. Absolom who was still pleading with his captain, Lord Harris, to let him have one more over.

Charles Absolom was a great character and a most valuable cricketer as well as the hero of many stories. A tireless man, he was known to arrive for a match having walked twelve miles, carrying his bag of gear, having breakfasted on a quart of beer and a pint of gooseberries. A wonderful story of him, which bears telling, concerns his off the field activities. At haymaking time he once hired himself to a farmer for five shillings (25p) a day plus his beer. It was said that he did the work of two men but, next day, the farmer, with tears in his eyes, pleaded with him to accept ten shillings (50p) a day and buy his own beer which, in those days, was no more than a penny (½p) a pint. His end was a sad one. He died in great agony at Port of Spain, Trinidad, in 1889 through being crushed by a crane which gave way whilst he was helping to discharge a cargo of sugar from the S.S. Muriel, of which he was purser. During the last ten years of his life he travelled extensively in America and was adopted by the Spokane Indians who gave him a name which meant 'the man who never wears a hat'.

TOM ADAMS,
one of the early characters
of Kent cricket, he also founded
the Bat & Ball ground, Gravesend.

Another great character and prominent member of the 'old Kent eleven' was Tom Adams. It was said that 'with a curl on each side under his hat and looking as though he had eaten live birds for breakfast . . . he was as bright as a first-class lark, upright as a roach and a very good man for his side . . . a first rate game shot and good at the trap; formerly very clever with his bunch of fives, but never quarrelsome, and may be summed up as a thorough good English cricketer'. Richard Daft in his 'Reminiscences of Cricket' said that Adams used to declare that he would achieve perfect happiness 'if he could play with a team who would stop at the wickets for three days, keep the opposite eleven in the field and, at the end of the third day, wish them good evening and thank them for a pleasant game'. A prize fighter once challenged Adams to box, shoot and play cricket for, a then, considerable purse, the boxing to take place first and the winner of two events be entitled to the stakes.

THIS year the club engaged the ground at St. Lawrence, which is still used. Fuller Pilch had the care of the ground and had got it into capital order.

The Cricket Week commenced on the 2nd August, in splendid weather, but owing to the General Election taking place at the time, some of the leading families and visitors were absent.

The first match occupied 3 days, with the following score:—

ENGLAND.

1st innings.		2nd innings.	
W. Nicholson, Esq., c Felix	11	c Felix	21
Dean, c Felix	13	b Hillier	4
Box, b Hillier	0	c Felix	19
Guy, c Felix	1	b Martingell	17
Parr, b Mynn	9	c Martingell	16
Sewell, st. Dorrington	0	run out	0
Clarke, not out	10	c Fredericks	16
H. Fellowes, Esq., b Mynn	2	c Felix	5
R. Kynaston, Esq., c Hillier	0	b Hillier	19
Wisden, c Hillier	1	st. Dorrington	8
Lillywhite, c Felix	1	not out	1
Byes 3, wides 4	17	Byes 5, wides 3	8
	67		154

KENT.

1st innings.		2nd innings.	
Adams, c Wisden	19	b Lillywhite	11
W. Pilch, b Lillywhite	22	b Lillywhite	2
E. Bayley, Esq., b Clarke	19	not out	0
F. Pilch, b Lillywhite	40	b Lillywhite	1
Martingell, c Sewell	7	b Wisden	11
N. Felix, Esq., b Wisden	24	c and b Wisden	0
A. Mynn, Esq., not out	12	not out	16
Dorrington, b Lillywhite	11	c and b Wisden	0
Martin, b Wisden	1	c Dean	11
F. Fredericks, Esq., b Wisden	0		
Hillier, b Wisden	4		
Byes, 6, w.b. 7	13	Bye	1
	172		53

The Gentlemen's Match commenced on Thursday and concluded on Friday, with the following score—

GENTLEMEN OF KENT.

1st innings.		2nd innings.	
W. Mynn, hit wicket	0	c Nash	24
C. G. Whittaker, b Fellowes	8	b Fellowes	11
L. Bayley, c Baldwin	1	b Nash	0
N. Felix, not out	41	c R. Grimston	19
A. Mynn, b Latour	7	b Nash	3
S. Deacon, c Latour	11	b Fellowes	16
C. Harenc, run out	6	not out	13
E. Taswell, b Fellowes	4	b Fellowes	1
C. Randolph, st. Nicholson	1	b Fellowes	6
A. Harenc, st. Nicholson	2	b Fellowes	0
F. Fredericks, c Kynaston	0	c Nicholson	1
Bye 1, wide balls 4	5	Byes	5
	96		99

GENTLEMEN OF ENGLAND.

1st innings.		2nd innings.	
Captain Latour, run out	15	not out	10
Hon. R. Grimston, b A. Harenc	6	c Harenc	31
Hon. F. Grimston, c Fredericks	10	run out	0
W. Nicholson, run out	3	c W. Mynn	13
R. Kynaston, b A. Mynn	0		
H. Fellowes, c Harenc	51		
E. S. Hartopp, c Bayley	2		
C. Hoare, c Whittaker	8	not out	12
T. Nash, b A. Mynn	0		
W. Denison, not out	0		
J. L. Baldwin, absent			
	108		88

The band of the 39th Regiment played on the ground each afternoon.

The scorecard of the first Canterbury cricket week matches to be played on the St Lawrence ground 1847.

The 'pugulist' had arranged, in his own mind, to give Adams so severe a beating in the boxing that he would be unable to take part in the other two events. Adams however, had other ideas for, when the prize fighter bore down on him, he went down without a blow and was counted out, remarking to his baffled opponent 'there, you have won that one'. Adams went on to win the shooting and the cricket with ease to claim the purse. He will however, best be remembered as the founder of the 'Bat and Ball' ground at Gravesend where Kent played many matches between 1849 and 1971.

Such stories and characters are as much part of the 'Week' and its history as the cricket itself to which we now return. During the course of 150 years and almost 300 matches it is inevitable that there should have been many close and exciting finishes. As far back as 1850, the Gentlemen of Kent required 165 to beat the Gentlemen of England. At close of play on the second day they were 40/6. Next morning Nicholas Felix and the Hon. E. V. Bligh made a stand which saw their side home by one wicket. Another exciting finish was against Surrey in George Hearne's benefit match in 1890. Surrey were the champion county that year and were making their first appearance in the 'Week'. Kent began their second innings 38 in arrears. Alec Hearne and L. A. H. Hamilton put on 78 for the first wicket and Leslie Wilson helped add 75 for the second. At close of play on Friday − the second day − the

Kent v Lancashire at Canterbury 1906, the year that Kent won the County Championship title for the first time in their history.

score stood at 158/2, Alec Hearne 72 not out. However, next morning he was out without addition to his score and, of the remaining batsmen, only W. H. Patterson was able to play the bowling of Lohmann with confidence and Surrey were left three hours and fifty minutes to get 191, on a drying wicket under a hot sun, against Fred Martin and Walter Wright, two of the finest left-arm bowlers of the day. With fifty minutes left for play they were 111/8 but Henry Wood, the wicket-keeper and former Kent player, stayed with Lohmann for forty minutes. Sharpe, who only had one eye, was last man in and had to face the last ball of the match from Martin. It completely beat him but went just about an inch above the stumps enabling Surrey to draw the match, still 48 runs behind.

Three times between 1908 and 1927 Hampshire were involved in sensational finishes. In 1908 their last pair, Stone and Newman, came together needing 51 to win with fifty minutes remaining. A win for Kent seemed almost certain but one or two catches went down and they got the runs with five minutes to spare. At the tea interval on the second day of the 1926 match, Hampshire, 268 behind, were 57/6. Most thought that half an hour next day would be enough to finish the match. In fact it went on until just before time on the last day. J. P. Parker, almost unknown to most people on the ground, battled fearlessly and, at the other end, Mead was playing the type of innings well remembered by regular spectators of the 'Week'. When play ended on the second day they had added 194 and, before Parker was out on the last day for 156, had taken their stand to 270 in two hours and fifty minutes. However, this was not the end of Kent's problems. Livesey assisted in a stand of 84 for the ninth wicket while Mead carried his bat for 175 leaving Kent a little over two hours to make 172. It took a magnificent stand of 135, in little more than an hour, by A. P. F. Chapman and F. E. Woolley, to make it possible.

In the following year, 1927, the excitement was less prolonged but the finish was possibly more dramatic. On the last day Hampshire were forced to follow-on 306 behind, but once again, Mead battled for more than four hours in an effort to save the match. When the last man, Boyes, went in the scoreboard read 234/9 and the result was still in the balance. Mead was facing when the last over was started and interest in the match had all but died. By the time the last ball was due to be bowled most of the crowd were leaving. 'Tich' Freeman was the bowler. Mead played for the ball to come straight on but it was the 'Googly'. It went off the edge to slip where Woolley, as so often before, completed the catch. Very few people had realised what had happened and left the ground without knowing the result.

For prolonged excitement and the bearing it had on the championship, it would be extremely difficult to better the Middlesex match of 1920. At the time Kent were in a very good position to secure the championship, with Middlesex unlikely contenders. At the end of the first day's play Kent, in reply to a Middlesex total of 212, were 163/1. However, during the night it rained and on the second day Nigel Haig, the Middlesex captain, gave his best bowling performance, up to that time, restricting Kent to a lead of only 5. Middlesex, in their second innings, lost six wickets in scoring 47, Freeman performing a hat trick, and the lead of only five began to look good enough. However, G. T. S. Stevens assisted Patsy Hendren to recover. When the innings finally closed Kent were left with a target of 123. At 70/1, with Bickmore and Seymour batting well, matters appeared well in hand. Things then began to go wrong. Seymour played a typical lofted hit to leg and was well caught by C. H. Gunasekera. Jack Hearne, bowling off breaks in bad light, bowled extremely well and wickets began to tumble rapidly. When bad light eventually brought an early end to play Kent were perilously placed at 94/6. Next day the total was taken to 107 before L. H. W. Troughton, the Kent captain, was out and, with only four added G. E. C. Wood's wicket fell. Bill Fairservice and Humphreys added six more leaving only six for victory. At this point Fairservice, trying to get away from Hearne's bowling, called Humphreys for a quick single, had they made it the match would probably have been won, but he was run out by Hendren. 'Tich' Freeman was cleaned bowled and Middlesex had gained an astonishing victory by five runs. By winning the remaining seven matches Middlesex went on to become champion county that season.

The last of these exciting finishes concerns the Lancashire match in 1956. They came to Canterbury as leading county while Kent were firmly implanted at the foot of the table — they finished in sixteenth position that season with only four wins. Lancashire's batting on the first day was disappointing and they managed to total only 258. A magnificent 121 from Colin Cowdrey, the first hundred scored against Lancashire that season, ensured Kent a lead of 38. In their second innings Lancashire lost Wharton and Washbrook before they cleared the arrears. On the last day they lost their remaining eight wickets for 112. Kent were left with a target of 119 in two hours and a quarter under darkening skies. Cowdrey and Arthur Phebey gave them a tremendous start and, despite a devastating spell of bowling by Brian Statham, they got home with three minutes to spare.

COLIN COWDREY who emulated Lord Harris in leading the side for fifteen years 1957-1971. It was he who led the side to the championship title in 1970.

Not only has the 'Week' provided some exciting and close finishes to matches it has also witnessed many fine individual performances. Perhaps the greatest of these was that played by Joe Hardstaff for Nottinghamshire in 1937. Bryan Valentine, the Kent captain, had declared Kent's second innings at 242/9 to leave Notts a target of 310 for victory in three and three quarter hours, an asking rate in excess of 80 per hour. The declaration appeared to be reasonable until Hardstaff, with a stream of handsome strokes compiled a hundred in 51 minutes. He made 117 out of 134 for the third wicket in an hour. His innings of 126 in seventy minutes was probably the fastest sustained scoring in the history of the 'Week' up to this time. It was also the foundation of a remarkable victory for his side with 45 minutes to spare.

Kent C.C.C. 1970. The side that brought the championship title to the county for the first time in 57 years.

An innings that surely deserves recording in this story of the 'Week' was that of Les Ames in the match against Middlesex in 1950. It was the match in which he recorded his 100th hundred in first-class cricket, thus becoming the second Kent player and only the 12th in the history of the game, to achieve this feat. Middlesex started the match with a stand of 99 between Robertson and Dewes and, with a splendid 62 from Sharp, they finally totalled 249. When Kent began their reply, Arthur Fagg was unlucky to be run out after hitting 88 out of 106 for the first wicket with Tony Pawson. It was

26

Kent and Leicestershire line up in front of the New Stand to be presented to H.R.H. The Duke of Kent 1986.

(a) *(b)*

BRIAN LUCKHURST (a) and MIKE DENNESS (b) probably the finest opening pair in the history of the club.

good enough to ensure a small lead for Kent before the declaration. Bill Edrich, the Middlesex captain, responded by declaring the second innings of Middlesex at 241/3 setting Kent a target of 237 to win. Fagg's wicket fell without a run on the board, which allowed Ames to come to the wicket. He played a grand innings, often running to drive, getting 131 out of 211 in two hours. He eventually fell to Moss, holding a hard drive close to the ground. Aside from his personal achievement he had laid the foundations for a Kent victory.

The 1990 'Week' commenced on Wednesday 25th July and ended on Tuesday 31st July — the first occasion in its long history that the festival 'week', or some part of it, had not been played in August. Although every effort had been made by the county club Committee to get the dates changed nothing could be done to accommodate the club and the original dates had to stand. None of this however was to detract from the traditional festive atmosphere and gaiety of the 'Week'.

ALAN EALHAM who succeeded the Late Colin Page as director of Youth coaching in the County.

The crowd absorbed in the play. Canterbury Week 1991.   *(Photo Mrs. Pat Fitch)*

Middlesex were the visitors for the first match and they came as leaders of the County Championship table and fresh from their conquest over Somerset in a third day run chase. Despite Kent's lowly position in the table a very good crowd were to witness a match that produced some fine individual performances and an exciting finish. Put in to bat after losing the toss, Kent suffered their first set-back with the fall of Mark Benson's wicket with the score at 83. Neil Taylor (152*) joined Simon Hinks (254) in establishing a new second wicket record stand of 366 – it was also a record for any Kent wicket in first-class cricket. On the way both batsmen passed their thousand runs for the season and Hinks recorded his highest score in first-class cricket. When Hinks' wicket fell on the second morning at 449, Mark Benson, the Kent captain, immediately declared Kent's innings. Middlesex began their reply by losing the wicket of Desmond Haynes, bowled Alan Iggleseden, with the score at 12. Mike Gatting then joined Mike Roseberry in a second wicket stand of 109 before Gatting was out for 52. Mark Ramprakash came to the wicket in a very determined mood but he lost Roseberry (82) with the score now at 155. Ramprakash (100*) and Keith Brown (57*) proceeded in great style to put on 153 for the fourth wicket and when Ramprakash reached his hundred Mike Gatting declared the Middlesex innings at 308/3, 141 behind. Kent, as so often in the past, began to lose wickets to some fine bowling by John Embury (3/3 in nine overs) and Norman Cowans (3/20 in ten overs) with Neil Williams giving good support with 3/65. Kent could only make 140. Middlesex were left to score 282 to win.

However, the excitement was not yet over. Desmond Haynes was bowled by Fanie de Villiers for nought and Roseberry fell to the same bowler l.b.w. for 14. With the scoreboard reading 23/2 the hope of Kent supporters began to rise. Mike Gatting (101) and Mark Ramprakash (125) put Middlesex back in contention with a stand of 198 for the third wicket. It was Ramprakash's second hundred of the match and he became only the sixth player in the history of the 'Week' to achieve this feat. When they were both out Kent bounced right back into the game, the next five wickets falling for 50 runs. When stumps were finally drawn Kent were two wickets away from victory and Middlesex six runs. It was indeed a wonderful match in keeping with festival cricket.

We have read of exciting and close finishes and of fine individual performances, but there is one other aspect of the story of the 'Week' which bears the telling, big hits. In the long list of big hits made during matches of the 'Week' the longest is reported to be that of Charles Inglis Thornton with a carry of 152 yards while playing for the South against the North in 1871. Before this however, in 1869 he hit every ball of a four ball over beyond the ring but in those days this only counted four and not six as today. There was then A. C. Watson of Sussex who, in 1925, cleared the tents at one end and the wooden stand, which then stood to the south of the pavilion, at the other. However, the blow that probably gave him most satisfaction was the one which scattered the tea cups in the tent of his host, Lord Lewisham. The ball was lost but eventually recovered during the winter behind a hedge with a piece of china still buried in it.

One big hit which will probably never be forgotten was made by J. L. Bryan of Kent during his innings of 236 against Hampshire in the 'Week' of 1933. It was a skimming drive which just swerved round the end of the sightscreen, through an open window of the pavilion and, on landing, struck the edge of a table with a shattering blow, and flew up into a picture of the 1877 cricket week. When the ball was retrieved it still had glass embedded in it and a fresh one had to be used when the game resumed. (The actual ball, still bearing its scars and suitably mounted, has been presented to the Club).

Despite all this however, the 'Week' has not been without its problems, including dissatisfaction and complaints against the

Umpires, as the following letter reveals. It was written by Sir
Frederick Ponsonby-Fane of the M.C.C. in the mid-nineteenth
century, to the secretary of the Kent club.

March 3rd '52

Dear Sir,

I said I would write to you on the subject of the Canterbury
Cricket matches previous to the season of '52 and, although it is
rather early to think of the game, it is perhaps as well that I should
be prepared to make some proposal as to continuing the matches
at Canterbury when the Committee of the M.C.C. meets. I know
that all members of the M.C.C. Committee are anxious to avoid any
differences with other clubs but at the same time I must say that
there was dissatisfaction with the course taken last year in
reference to umpires, so much so that many members were in
favour of making the matches with the Gentlemen who proposed
to take them up in other parts of Kent.

The M.C.C. have no wish to gain advantage in a game but
consider it for the interest of the game that M.C.C. umpires should
be employed in the great matches. The constant applications
which they receive to allow their men to be umpiring in county
games shows that there is a feeling of confidence in those men. It
was at the particular request of the Kent committee that the M.C.C.
broke their rule a few years ago by allowing the match at
Canterbury, Gents v Gents, to be played with only one M.C.C.
umpire. In making these observations I do not mean to doubt the
honesty and capacity of the umpires but, having to deal with many
different clubs, the M.C.C. find it best to adhere to their own rule. If
it is wished that the matches be played as usual in London and
Canterbury, I shall be very glad to support that proposition
provided it is understood that M.C.C. umpires are to be employed
having, however, as heretofore, the agreement as to one umpire at
Canterbury in the Gentlemen's match. I should be much obliged to
you for an answer as early as you can manage to give me one and I
can only say that having been the first person to support the
transfer of matches from Town Malling (now West Malling) to
Canterbury I should be sorry to see it come to an end.

I remain yours
Fred'k Ponsonby

By 1849 there were also player problems creeping in as we see from the following letter written by Edward Gower Wenman who was a very prominent member of the 'good old Kent eleven'.

Benenden
August 4th 1849

Sir,

In consequence of my determination to retire from the cricket ground I have had no practice for a long time and had persuaded myself that I had sunk into a state of obscurity from which I was not likely to be call'd — I much regret that the honour of Kent seems on the wane but feel myself quite unable to do anything to retrieve it. I would much prefer remaining in my present obscurity to again taking the field — yet from the pressing invitations I have received from different quarters I will for once consent to do my best, fearing however, that you will receive nothing from my exertions but disappointment.

Your most obedient servant
E. G. Wenman

In 1852 he again wrote as follows:

Benenden
August 2nd '52

Sir,

I shall be afraid to make an attempt at cricket as I get no practice and still get older (at this time Wenman was 49). I shall do no good but will endeavour to try once more and meet my old friends at the time required.

I am Sir,
Your obedient servant
E. G. Wenman

Despite these letters of gloom Wenman continued playing until 1854 when he finally retired.

These things alone cannot explain the success and popularity of a festival 'Week' that has survived two world wars and many changes in our habits and way of life. It became 'the thing to do' to go to

Canterbury Week, and it has ever remained so. There is still much of the atmosphere and spirit of the past in that it is one of the few remaining places where 'straw boaters' are still worn with the colours of 'I.Z.' and 'B.B.' on their bands. These colours however, are not restricted to male members, for I.Z. allow wives, daughters and sisters to wear them as do B.B. These traditions in dress are accompanied by similar traditions in entertainment.

CHAPTER 2

The Social Side

HOSPITALITY in the tents was very generous before the outbreak of the Second World War in 1939 and even today it is surprising how much of it has survived. Perhaps there are not quite so many tents today as in the earliest days, when pictures show them half way round the ground, but I.Z. O.S. and B.B., The Buffs, the leading Canterbury Clubs and the Mayor, still have their tents as do the President of the Club and the High Sheriff of the County, together with numerous commercial organisations. The hospitality ensures renewal of old friendships, for the 'Week' is one of those occasions where you are certain to meet, at some time, those acquaintances you never see from one year to the next.

From the year of its formation until 1870 the arrangements for the 'Week' were the responsibility of the Beverley Club which, at different times, was known as the 'Beverley Kent Club' or 'The East Kent Cricket Club' and, for a short time 'The Kent Cricket Club'. The first appointed secretary was W. M. Smithson who was succeeded by Wiliam de Chair Baker in 1849. He was the brother of John Gerrard Baker, the founder of the club.

The management of the 'Week' remained in the hands of the Beverley club even when the County club was formed in 1859 with W. de Chair Baker seemingly in sole charge. It was a very difficult position only resolved when the Kent County Club and the Beverley Club amalgamated in 1870 to become the present Kent County Cricket Club. W. de Chair Baker was named as the first Honorary secretary of the new club and continued to manage the 'Week' until his death in 1888.

Lord Harris, who took over as secretary, said of de Chair Baker, 'he was the most friendly of companions and the kindest of souls — devoted to the game and his county'. Much credit for the establishment of the 'Week' as one of the greatest institutions in the English cricket season is due to him. Although Lord Harris took over as secretary the management of the 'Week' passed to Captain Geoffrey Austin and, when he died in 1902, to the secretary/ manager and eventually the secretary and committee of the County club.

An artist's impression of the entrance to the ground in 1892 and a photograph taken in 1953. In the photograph the Bat & Ball public house is hidden on the left.

For over 120 years the history of the 'Week' has run parallel to the history of the County cricket club and, whenever that is mentioned, one name stands out above all others. George Robert Canning Harris. There are few alive today who recognise the extent of his achievements for the club. He first played for Kent in 1870 when its cricket had sunk to a very low ebb. There were many good, qualified amateurs around but they showed very little interest or enthusiasm in playing for the county, preferring to enjoy country house cricket which, in those days, was very prominent.

Among those amateurs were C. J. Ottaway, a very sound batsman who played in the 'Week' on only two occasions – Alfred Lubbock, another fine player who played only four times in twelve years, and his brother Edgar who appeared only once. The side relied on the professionals Edgar Willsher and George 'Farmer' Bennett who were both nearing the end of their careers, with the assistance of anyone who could be found, amateur or professional. Nine matches were played in 1864 and all were lost, which led to Kentish folk taking little interest in the fortunes of the county side.

Lord Harris was to be the man responsible for lifting the County Club from this depression and restoring the interest of its following. He captained the side from 1875 till 1889 and, beside being a brilliant fielder and useful change bowler, was, for a very long time, the best batsman in the side. He was Honorary secretary from 1875 until 1880 and President in 1875, thus becoming the only man to be Secretary, Captain and President at one and the same time, an occurrence that, of course, can never be repeated.

The City 'en fete' for the Jubilee 'Week' 1891.

Hop Oasts and players' tents in the days before the pavilion was built. The hop oasts can still be seen behind the practice nets but have now been converted into flats.

A familiar scene on Ladies Day, be-decked in all their finery the ladies bask in the shade of the tree, and promenade during the interval to the strains of the military band.

In a very short space of time he persuaded the best of the amateurs to assist the County side whenever they could but, more importantly, to play in the 'Week' which was, in those days and remains today, an honour. He also did a great deal to foster amateur cricket in the county by reviving the 'Band of Brothers' whilst persevering in his search for promising professionals and all the time ensuring the very high standard of behaviour, both on and off the field, which has for long been a county tradition.

The great days of Kent cricket were restored with the founding of the Tonbridge nursery in 1897 by which time the playing career of Lord Harris was over. However, he continued to remain active behind the scenes, being Chairman of the Managing Committee and a Trustee, until his death in 1932. He was held in great respect for his judgement, be it on cricket or other matters. No man did more to make and keep the 'Week' what it is.

Of all the sides that have represented Kent in matches of the 'Week' it would be difficult to name a more attractive and stronger one than that which took the field in 1906. The side, in batting order, read: E. W. Dillon, C. J. Burnup, Seymour, K. L. Hutchings, J. R. Mason, Humphreys, R. N. R. Blaker, C. H. B. Marsham, Huish, Blythe and Fielder. It was also a brilliant fielding side with an array of slips second to none among the first-class counties. The visitors for that 1906 'Week' were Sussex and Lancashire, neither of whom could be described as weak teams. Against Sussex, Kent made a formidable 568 at a rate in excess of 100 an hour and won the match by an innings and 131 runs. The Lancashire side, which included such great players as R.H. Spooner, A. C. MacLaren and J. T. Tyldesley, were also beaten by an innings and 195 runs. Such was the strength of the Kent side that year that Frank Woolley, who had already proved his worth as a match-winner, could not secure a place in the 'Week'.

The 'Jubilee Week' was celebrated in 1891. Gloucestershire and Surrey were the visitors and, the weather being very wet and dismal over the first four days, both matches were drawn. Barrauds of Oxford Street published a photograph of the leading people identified with the 'Week', which numbered around 300. The Mayor's banquet to the Old Stagers and the Kent County Cricket Club on the Wednesday evening was a brilliant success with some very good speeches by Earl Stanhope, the Earl of Winchilsea and Nottingham, Sir Spencer Ponsonby-Fane and the Earl of Darnley. The general decorations were carried out by the London specialists, Paine and Son. Venetian masts bearing shields and flags made a continual line from both railway stations to the St Lawrence ground. A military band played in the Dane John gardens each evening, local friendly societies arranged torchlight processions and the Cycle Club organised a lantern ride. Many of the residents also decorated their houses so that the city never before presented a more colourful appearance.

Luckily the rain ceased each evening so that the streets were thronged with sightseers and a vast crowd witnessed the display of fireworks on Babs Hill on the Thursday evening. Outside the Old Theatre a wonderful scene was set and among the many songs was one sung by the Spirit of Jubilee, the concluding verse of which was:

The First Day of the
Canterbury Week.

1 The Pitch was not marked till
       1 o'clock,

2 And after the spectators had waited
   with the most exemplary patience for
       another two hours,

3 F.M.G. made the toss, and
   the game was finally commenced
       by

4 Ferris 2,

5 Braybrooke.

Some scenes of the first day of the 1891 'Week'.

'and these are ladies, bless their hearts,
who charmingly play the female parts,
And applaud the cricketers brave and bold,
Whose prowess needn't here be told.
Likewise recruits of later age,
Like those appearing on the stage,
to help the little original set,
Of famed O.S. remaining yet.
upon the spot we choose for you,
To see the '91 review
Of the Spirit of Jubilee.

Toward the end of the epilogue Mr Loraine Baldwin, a famous Old Stager himself then in his eighty-fourth year, presented each of the actresses with a bouquet after which Miss Carlotta Anderson, as the Spirit of O.S., rendered the following lines:

'A truce to fearful chords in minor key,
In the glad paean of our Jubilee,
This consolation we can count upon,
Men come and go and still O.S. go on.
When (ere its innings at an end shall be)
The cricket week completes its century.
O.S. will do the same without a doubt,
Both comrades 'going strong' and still "not out".

The Centenary Week should have been celebrated in 1941, but, due to the Second World War, was delayed until 1948. What a difference there was on this occasion compared to the Jubilee Week! Now there were no street decorations or bands in the Dane John gardens in the evenings and no special events were organised. There was not even a dinner or banquet to honour the occasion. We can only assume that since the Jubilee Week there had been two devastating world wars that had changed people's habits to such a degree as to make them oblivious of such a great event. Other factors which lent a hand were the fact that at this time there was still a degree of rationing and such festivities would have been difficult to stage. Even clothing and household linens still required coupons before they could be purchased. Perhaps we had not yet fully recovered from the austerity of the war years.

The weather too was similar to that for the Jubilee Week, wet, dull and miserable and this was reflected in the attendances for only 26,365 were present for the week as opposed to 46,756 the previous year. Hampshire and Nottinghamshire were the visitors and, as in the Jubilee week, both matches were drawn.

The military band entertain the tent holders during the tea interval. These days they do not play throughout the day as in the past.

Despite all this however, there were things that had not changed. The St Lawrence ground took on its air of festival with the huge semi-circle of tents and marquees set out on one side of the ground, all with their identifying flags above them as one hundred years before. The Old Stagers, I. Zingari, Band of Brothers, The Mayor, the East Kent and Canterbury Clubs, the Conservative Club and the Buffs. A military band also played but now only on the first day and on Ladies Day and the ever-present Old Stagers still staged their theatricals each evening as they had done since those early days in 1842.

The spirit and traditions of the 'Week' had also survived. The 'Week' could never be described as simply a "quaint survival" of the past for, throughout its history, it has preserved much of what was good in the old while never ceasing to take in much of what is good in the new – as it will no doubt do during its continuing history.

When in 1841 the decision was taken to hold a cricket week in the following year, it was resolved it should also be 'A Grand

Festival Week', with cricket being the principal attraction. And this is exactly what it turned out to be.

In the City the long narrow High Street was bright with bunting and coloured lamps, becoming an avenue of colour. Every other house had window boxes filled with flowers and plants, the Scarlet and Blue of the men of the garrison in the streets and the summer dresses of the ladies all adding to the wealth of colour. All the drapers and tailors shops decorated their windows with the ribbons of 'I. Zingari' and the 'Band of Brothers'. With a blue sky above, sunshine and the presence of the mighty cathedral, there was nowhere, at home or abroad, to compare with the majesty and beauty of Canterbury in its festival week.

As for the ground itself the scene is perhaps best set by Lt.Col. Newnham-Davis in 'The History of Kent County Cricket' (Eyre and Spottiswoode 1907) wherein he relates:
"Making the journey from the city by 'Fly' (1) we drive past the market place (2) through sleepy St Georges Place, which bestirs itself for the 'Week'. Over the railway bridge past the sheltered villas and down the little avenue of limes to the gate where a crowd of lookers-on and gentlemen of no occupation cluster. Announcements of comfortable teas to be obtained in gardens and safe shelter for bicycles are hung out on old pink garden walls and from doors of comfortable old cottages. Up a little hill, where a man takes the tickets, and we are on the ground".

Describing the scene still further he goes on to say:
"Somebody, somewhere in print, has called Canterbury Week the Goodwood of cricket and the first sight of the great array of tents, the flags, the carriages and the moving crowds does suggest a racecourse. To the right towers the pavilion. Just before us on a gentle mound, are lines of interested spectators with behind them carriages and flys. A broad curve of canvas tents sweeps away to the left, a big tree marking its centre. Beyond again are more carriages and 'drags' (3). Next, a large stand before we reach a raised bank and another curve of seated spectators. Each little enclosure in front of the tents is as bright as a flower bed with the summer dresses of the ladies. Among the crowds on the benches too there is a mass of colour, for the 'fair maids of Kent and Kentish maids' love to watch a cricket match. The garrison has come down in force, both the Cavalry and the County Regiment, 'The Buffs', to see the County eleven play. Space in the semi-circle given over to

42

The famous Lime tree that stands within the boundary of the St. Lawrence ground. (Photo by Anthony Roberts)

the tents is eagerly applied for and should any holder of frontage, by descriptive right, give up that right there are many requests for the vacant position".

Continuing to set the scene he further adds:
"Let us now take it that a great shout has announced the last wicket of an innings is down and follow the multitudes into the oval of the inner ground and look around. The flags that flutter on the ridges of the marquees or from great staffs, will show us who, in most cases, occupy them. Black, Red and Gold tell us that that tent is reserved for 'I. Zingari' and their friends. Further along, many Kentish flags amid this small village of tents mark the Mayor and corporation, another Black, Red and Gold catches the eye and the great 'O.S.' on it in white letters shows us that it is the abiding place of the Old Stagers. This tent at tea time is always the meeting place for those who are of the world of theatre. Next a light barrier, wound about with Buff and Blue, marks the lawn before the tent of the 'Buffs', the East Kent Regiment, and N.C.O's in scarlet and Buff facings stand guard at the entrance (4). The Band of Brothers,

Every two years retired capped players are invited to spend a day of the 'Week' as guests of the club. This picture taken in 1990 shows from left to right: Doug Wright; Eddie Crush; Alan Dixon; David Nicholls; Peter Foster; J. F. Pretlove; 'Hopper' Levett; Colin Fairservice; Les Ames; Richard Hills; Claud Lewis; Arthur Phebey; Godfrey Evans; Alan Shireff; Derek Underwood; Geoff Smith; Bob Wilson and Brian Luckhurst. In the wheelchair: G. L. Bryan.

further along the curve, show off with Blue and Black bunting. There too are the tents of the East Kent and Canterbury clubs together with the local Conservative club".

This then is the scene which greeted the vast crowds attracted to the Grand Festival Week. But, as has been said, the 'Week' was also to provide entertainment and amusement for those visitors to the cricket who would be remaining in the city for the whole week, and this was not forgotten.

After stumps were drawn for the day Canterbury and all within the city rested until the evening which brought with it a choice of entertainment. There were guest nights at the barracks, for most of the county people who stayed in Canterbury were in hotels or other lodgings. The Old Stagers played at the theatre on Monday, Tuesday, Thursday and Friday, alternating two programmes. On Wednesday and Friday the County Balls took place. One of several bands engaged for the 'Week' played each evening in the Dane John gardens and there was always music elsewhere in the city. A small troupe of entertainers, pierrots or wandering minstrels, generally established themselves somewhere on the outskirts of

A quintet of Kent wicketkeepers; Godfrey Evans; Les Ames; 'Hopper' Levett; Alan Knott and Steve Marsh.

the city for the 'Week' and there were the illuminated streets to wonder at nightly. Let us once again read the descriptive words of Lt.Col. Newnham-Davis.

"No town is more suitable than Canterbury for evening decoration. The old gate (Westgate Towers) at the end of the long street is outlined by twinkling lines of light. The Corn Exchange, the Beaney Institute and the Guildhall all shine with electricity. All down the High Street little coloured electric lights are strung overhead from house to house. The Buttermarket flames with light, Mercury Lane glows like a casket of jewels for, across the narrow street where great Tudor houses seem to lean forward to touch each other, Japanese lanterns are hung and the space between the buildings is full of luminous colour. Equally beautiful are the effects where the dark stream, a branch of the river (Stour) slips under the bridge by the house of the Canterbury Weavers, the reflection of multi-coloured lanterns and the devices of light quiver in the silent, flowing water. Canterbury, beautiful at all times, is not least beautiful when she puts on all her jewels for a gala night".

Sadly it could not last forever. The intervention of two world wars, the expansion and development of the railways and other forms of public transport followed by the coming of the motor car brought inevitable changes. There were too, the changing social habits of those who came to see the cricket, all of which contributed to the age old traditions of the 'Week' fading into memory. The greatest of these changes will be noticed in the city, for no longer are to be seen the bunting, illuminations and decorations, and apart from the Old Stagers, who still present their theatricals each night at the local theatre, there is no other entertainment for the few who still stay in Canterbury for the 'Week'. The cost of decorating and illuminating the city would, in these days, be prohibitive, the more so as the city does not attract the number of people who will take up residence for the whole of the 'Week'. As social habits changed so did the type of function that was provided. Patronage of the County Balls faded and these were among the first to be discontinued.

However, today's visitors will see little change when they arrive at the St Lawrence Ground. As they enter the ground they will still see the huge semi-circle of colourful tents and marquees sweeping away to the left. Still will be seen those of the Mayor, The East Kent and Canterbury clubs, the local Conservative club, the Regimental flag of the Buffs but not the N.C.O.'s guarding the entrance as of old for no longer is the Regimental Silver laid out in the tent; it remains safely back in the barracks. There too are still to be seen the Black Red and Gold of I. Zingari and the ever present Black and Blue of the Band of Brothers. The Old Stages still proudly fly their flag, albeit from a shared tent today.

These days spectators arrive at the ground not by 'drag' or 'fly' but by motor car and it is these which occupy the raised banking and other areas where once stood horse drawn carriages. Military bands no longer play throughout the day every day of the 'Week'. Today, on the days they do appear, they give a display of marching and counter-marching on the outfield during the lunch and tea intervals.

There is however, one grand tradition that is still maintained. Ladies Day, although not on the scale of yesteryear and the golden days of the 'Week', is beginning to take on some of the glory of the past. From the very beginnings of the 'Week' Thursday was always set aside as 'Ladies Day'. Tradition has it that on this day the lady visitors and guests would parade in their finery while the band played popular military airs during the intervals. It was a sight worthy of the Grand Festival that was the 'Week'. Like most others of the early traditions it began to fade after the second world war but concerted efforts by the County Committee and with the co-operation of the lady guests it is once more beginning to establish itself as the grandest day of the 'Week'. On this day all the gatemen can be seen wearing button-holes and, providing the sun is shining and the weather fair, no finer sight is to be seen. Such is the nature of the 'Week' that it will always adapt to modern times without losing sight of its origins.

(1) A 'fly' was a one horse hackney carriage.
(2) The market place was the old cattle market which is now the site of the Bus station.
(3) A 'drag' was a four-horsed carriage like a stage coach.
(4) The N.C.O's guarded the entrances to the tent where the Regimental silver was displayed during the 'Week'.

CHAPTER 3

The Old Stagers

THE history of 'Old Stagers' begins with the history of Canterbury Cricket Week. Conceived in the same year and born on the same day, they are part of the 'Week' and may truly be said to have had no existence away from Canterbury.

It was in 1842 that the Old Stagers first journeyed to Canterbury as amateur actors to appear at the Old Theatre in Orange Street. They were nearly all cricketers as well as amateur actors, and Canterbury was a place not unknown to many of them. This was however, the first occasion on which they had come as 'amateur rogues and vagabonds'. They had not yet styled themselves 'Old Stagers' and though they had no rules and regulations and the Black, Red and Gold ribbon they are entitled to wear during Canterbury Week had not yet been invented by their very good friends 'I. Zingari' (who were not formed until some years later) they were the original members of that band of amateur actors who, for the past 150 years, have 'trod the boards' during the festival Week, and who, cricketers or non-cricketers, may fairly lay claim to be remembered when men speak of Canterbury and cricket.

The Old Theatre in Orange Street, scene of the early performances of the Old Stagers.

But what is this connection with the 'Week' and its story? For this we must go back to the year 1839 when a 'Grand match' was arranged between Kent and England for the benefit of Fuller Pilch, to be played on his home ground at Town (now West) Malling. Among the names of those appearing in the England side are F. Ponsonby and C. G. Taylor. Again, in 1840, we find the name of C. G. Taylor among those playing for the Beverley Club against their old rivals from Chilston. In 1841 both Ponsonby and Taylor were in the England side that opposed Kent at Canterbury.

The interest in these matches was so great that John Baker, the moving spirit behind the Beverley Club, suggested to Ponsonby, who was also a well known amateur actor, that in the following year not only should the cricket matches be played but that he and some of his Cambridge friends, also amateur actors, should perform at the Canterbury Theatre in Orange Street in the evenings for the entertainment of visitors to the cricket who would be remaining in the City for the whole week. Ponsonby and Taylor took up the idea with great enthusiasm and before they left Canterbury the preliminary details were settled.

By the following year all had fitted nicely into place and on the evening of Monday, 1st August 1842, the first day of the very first Canterbury Cricket Week, the curtain rose on the first of the many performances given by the Old Stagers throughout the years. An amateur band attended, conducted by the celebrated Kent cricketer of the day, Nicholas Felix (real name Wanostrocht). On the first night, they presented "The Poor Gentleman" followed on Tuesday by Sheridan's "The Rivals". On Thursday and Friday the plays were "Too Late For Dinner" and "Othello Travestie".

The whole week was a complete success, both on the cricket field and in the theatre, as confidently predicted by John Baker. The Canterbury newspapers were full of praise for the amateur actors. So great was the success it made certain that the 'Week' would be held again the following year. That it has in fact lasted for 150 years supports the wisdom of those early pioneers.

The amateur cricketers and actors had chosen The Fountain Hotel at which to stay. It soon became their headquarters and remained so until it was destroyed by fire during a bombing raid on the City in the 1939-1945 war. Two rooms were set aside for the Old Stagers while they were in residence for the 'Week', the door of one bearing the notice 'For The Old Stagers' and the other 'For Old Stagers Only'. The lettering of these notices is composed of human figures in contorted attitudes. We say 'is' because they are still in existence to this day.

The Fountain Hotel, Canterbury — headquarters of the Old Stagers when in Canterbury until it was destroyed by fire during the second world war.

The notice which was placed on the door of the Old Stagers room in The Fountain Hotel.

But to revert to 1842 and those first performances: the names of some taking part will be known to few. However, to identify some of them will serve to show the very strong association between the cricket and the theatricals.

There were Mr. T. A. Anson, the Hon. R. Grimston, Capt. P. Mundy, the Hon. F. Ponsonby, the Hon. S. Ponsonby and F. Thackeray, all of whom were members of the Gentlemen of England side who played against, and lost to, the Gentlemen of Kent in the second match of the 'Week'. The Hon. F. Ponsonby was also Captain of the England side that beat Kent in the first match, while the remainder of the side were professional. Nicholas Felix, who conducted the orchestra each evening, played for the Gentlemen of Kent.

Excitement abounded in 1843. The newly formed Kent Cricket Club played a match at Lord's against England, winning by three wickets. The return, played at Canterbury, was full of interest, Kent winning this time by nine wickets. The amateurs were seen again both on the cricket field and on the stage but now with some new names among their number, names that were to become very familiar in later years at Canterbury, W. Bolland, L. Hartop, R. Keate and others. Their true names did not appear on the programmes for it was customary then to adopt 'noms de theatre' which vaguely disguised their true identities. Apparently the reason for this was that it was thought not quite the thing for young men in the Learned Professions or Civil Service, making their way in the world, to play-act in public. However, the custom was discontinued in 1901 when, by common consent, the practice was dropped.

The following year, 1844, opened badly. A gale blew down the tents on the St Stephen's ground and the storm continued throughout the 'Week'. At the theatre the amateurs presented a somewhat different bill, the performances commencing with a prologue written by F. Ponsonby and W. Bolland. The first night's programme thereafter consisting of a two act farce 'The Haunted Inn'. This was followed by a comic interlude 'Sylvester Daggewood' and then a brand new 'Operatico Terpsicorean Burlesque', written for this anniversary, entitled 'Esmeralda'. The press account related:

> 'this piece abounds in appropriate witticisms on the passing events of the day, having allusion to several matters recently before the public connected with the sporting world, and deals out many severe "cuts" at the domestic policy of the existing government, of which some slashing hits at Peck and others, but more particularly at Sir James Graham, in reference to the Post Office espionage and the stopping of race course gangs.'

Although the newspaper goes on to say 'these hits were loudly applauded in all parts of the theatre, there were evidently some who took offence, though at what we are not told'. The burlesque was withdrawn on the last night and the entire cast assembled on stage to sing the National Anthem. W. Bolland made a speech explaining their action in deference to some 'busy tatlers' and assuring the audience that though conscious of no offence, they did not wish to risk causing any ill-will. Amends were made by a speech from the auditorium regretting the withdrawal, and so ended the one and only incident of its kind that has occurred during Canterbury Week.

Time and space does not allow the events of each succeeding year to be related, indeed it would be tedious and pointless to do so, but 1845 was a landmark of some importance for in July of that year, I. Zingari, of which we read more about in a subsequent chapter, was founded. W. Bolland was informed that he was to be Perpetual President and 20 of their friends were told that they were to be members. In an account given in later years by the founders, and printed at the beginning of the 'I.Z.' book of rules, they say "when at Cambridge, F. Ponsonby, C. G. Taylor, W. Bolland and others, devoted some of their leisure moments to cricket and theatricals. From this sprung many matches under various names, several theatrical meetings and finally, the annual Canterbury gatherings."

As we are told elsewhere, the name I. Zingari was adopted because they had no permanent home or cricket ground. As far as Canterbury was concerned these amateurs were both actors and cricketers. In fact of the twenty-five original members of I.Z. thirteen were also members of O.S., including the Perpetual President, the Annual Vice-President and five of the first biennial committee of six.

It was not until 1851, their tenth season, that the amateurs announced themselves on their playbills as 'The Old Stagers', and not until 1858 that any separate rules for 'O.S.' were recorded. However, separate records of the theatricals and the cricket matches were kept from the year 1842 and that year has always been regarded as the foundation year of Old Stagers. For their tenth season great efforts were made and the playbills proclaimed:

'Cricket Week 1851, tenth season. Great attraction, old faces, new pieces. The Old Stagers have the honour to inform the Nobility, Gentry and foreign visitors to the Great Exhibition, and the public in general, that their annual performances during the 'Week' will take place at the theatre in Canterbury'.

In 1891 the Jubilee of The Grand Festival Week was celebrated, and quite naturally the Old Stagers also celebrated this year as

CANTERBURY, 1842.

ON MONDAY, AUGUST 1, & ON THURSDAY, AUGUST 4,

Will be performed COLMAN's Comedy of

THE POOR GENTLEMAN.

CHARACTERS :

Sir Charles Cropland	C. ELLISON, Esq.	Lieutenant Worthington	TOM TAYLOR, Esq.
Sir Robert Bramble	M. G. BRUCE, Esq.	Frederick Bramble	C. G. TAYLOR, Esq.
Corporal Foss	G. C. BENTINCK, Esq.	Doctor Ollapod	Captain W. L. Y. BAKER.
Humphrey Dobbins	Hon. SPENCER PONSONBY.	Warner	H. HUDDLESTON, Esq.
Farmer Harrowby	T. ANSON, Esq.	Stephen Harrowby	Hon. F. PONSONBY.
	Valet ... F. THACKERAY, Esq.		
Miss Lucretia Mactab	Mrs. NISBETT.	Emily Worthington	Miss JANE MORDAUNT.
Dame Harrowby	M. G. BRUCE, Esq.	Mary	Miss WILLIAMS.

After which the Operatic Extravaganza entitled

OTHELLO TRAVESTIE !

Being the most excruciating Comic-Operatic-Tragedy that was ever tragedized by any Comical and Pastoral Company of Tragical Tragedians.

CHARACTERS :

Othello   (an independent Nigger, but a thought too jealous)   Hon. F. PONSONBY.

Iago   (from the Emerald Isle)   Hon. SPENCER PONSONBY.

Brabantio   (a *leetle* hasty)   G. BENTINCK, Esq.

Cassio   (a man of no note, except for liquor)   Captain BAKER.

Roderigo   (a silly youth, but partial to Mrs. Othello)   Captain P. MUNDY.

Duke of Venice   (partial to beer and tobacco, like many other dukes)   J. LORAINE BALDWIN, Esq.

Ludovico   (a decidedly respectable gentleman)   C. ELLISON, Esq.

First Policeman   (not given to unnecessary interference)   T. ANSON, Esq.

Second Policeman   (very like his comrade)   Hon. R. GRIMSTON.

LADIES :

Desdemona   (a *striking* beauty)   CHARLES G. TAYLOR, Esq.

Emilia   (her attendant)   M. G. BRUCE, Esq.

An Amateur Band will attend, under the superintendence of N. FELIX, Esq.

Doors will be opened at Seven o'clock.   Performances will commence at Quarter before Eight precisely.   Box Places may be secured daily, from Twelve o'clock till Four, of Miss ENGEHAM, Box Office, Theatre.   No one will be admitted without a Ticket ; and for the Boxes, places must be secured previous to the days of performance.   No remuneration whatever will be made to any Performer, nor will any money be received at the doors, or for Tickets.

☞ *The County Fancy Dress Ball will take place at Barnes's Assembly Rooms, on Wednesday Evening, August 3rd.   Tickets may be had of Mr. Ward, Bookseller, Mercery Lane, Canterbury.*

The playbill for the first Canterbury Week performances – 1842.

THEATRE ROYAL, CANTERBURY---AMATEUR THEATRICALS.

Cricket Week, 1851.   The Tenth Season ! ! ! ! ! ! ! ! ! !

GREAT ATTRACTION.   OLD FACES & NEW PIECES.

The " OLD STAGERS " have the honour to inform the Nobility, Gentry, Foreign Visitors to the Great Exhibition, and the Public in general, that their usual Performances during the Cricket Week, will take place at the Theatre at Canterbury,

On MONDAY August 11, TUESDAY August 12, THURSDAY August 14, FRIDAY August 15.

The following popular Dramatic Works have been selected for representation :—

HEARTS ARE TRUMPS.	NOT A BAD JUDGE.
JOHN DOBBS.	A NABOB FOR AN HOUR.
DEAF AS A POST!	THE LOTTERY TICKET.

Principal Characters by

Sir CHARLES CROPLAND, Bart.	The Hon. RICHARD ROE
The Hon. S. WHITEHEAD	JOHN DOE, Esq.
J. NOAKES, Esq.	E. EVANS, Esq.
H. PERCIVAL, Esq.	T. KNOX, Esq.
The CHEVALIER ESEOM	ALFRED MYNN, Esq.
J. LOLAINE, Esq.	&c., &c.
Mrs. A. WIGAN	Miss CATHCART
Mrs. CAULFIELD	Miss MARSTON.

The numerous and talented SMITH FAMILY have been engaged at an enormous expense, and will appear, reckless of consequences, every evening during the Season.

During the course of the Season various important Novelties in the Zoological Department will be produced, under the direction of the Chevalier ESEOM.

Apologist   ...   O. ADOLPHUS, Esq.   General Manager   ...   John DOE, Esq.
Stage Manager   ...   John NOAKES, Esq.
Musical Director   ...   Mr. MOUNT.   Leader of the Band   ...   Herr FELIX, R. S. V. P.
Substage Manager, Prompter, &c.   ...   Promiscuous SMITH, Esq.
Author and Composer   ...   J. NOAKES, Esq.

Boxes, 5s.   Pit, 2s.   Gallery, 1s.   Doors open at half-past Seven ; to commence at Eight.
The Box Plan is at Mr. Trimnell's, Parade.

Vivat Regina !

The playbill for the Jubilee 'Week' presentations – 1881

GREAT ATTRACTION.—OLD FACES AND NEW PIECES.

GORGEOUS NEW SCENERY AND SPLENDID DECORATIONS.

The "Old Stagers" have the honour to inform the Nobility, Gentry, Foreign Visitors to the Great Exhibition, and the Public in general, that

ON MONDAY, AUGUST 11, 1851,

The Performances will commence (by the kind permission of the Author, MARK LEMON, Esq.), with the successful Drama of

HEARTS ARE TRUMPS.

Mr. Gray   (under the assumed name of "Ruby," a hoary gambler)   The Hon. RICHARD ROE.
Captain Wagstaff   (a rook and a ruffian of polished exterior)   JOHN NOAKES, Esq.
Charles Wilmot   (a green and ingenuous young man)   H. PERCIVAL, Esq.
Mr. Goad   (an attorney, but a wretch)   T. KNOX, Esq.
Joe Martin   (a Yorkshire tyke)   JOHN DOE, Esq.
(His first appearance on the stage since his late severe accident).
Trotter   (Mr. Goad's clerk, occasionally in buttons)   The Chevalier ESROM.
Waiter ... The Hon. S. WHITEHEAD.   Gent ... A. MYNN, Esq.
Miss Gray ... Miss CATHCART.   Mrs. Fuller ... Mrs. COE.   Susan Fletcher ... Mrs. A WIGAN.
Guests, Waiters, &c., by the numerous and talented SMITH FAMILY.
Incidental to the piece, an air with variations will be executed on the violin by J. NOAKES, Esq.

———

After which will be presented (by the kind permission of the Author, J. M. MORTON, Esq., the favourite Comedietta, entitled

JOHN DOBBS!

Squire Fallowfield   (a stout and simple country gentleman)   M. BRUCE, Esq.
(His first appearance at Canterbury these two years.)
Major Frankman   (of her Majesty's service)   Sir C. CROPLAND, Bart.
Peter Paternoster   (a button manufacturer on a large scale)   E. EVANS, Esq.
John Dobbs   (a genius and a gentleman)   H. PERCIVAL, Esq.
John   (a footman)   J. LORRAINE, Esq.   James   (a footman)   The Chevalier ESROM.
Mrs. Chesterton   (a charming widow, daughter of the squire)   Miss. CATHCART.
Lucy   (her sister)   Miss J. MARSTON.

The Jubilee 'Week' playbill

55

their Jubilee year. The Mayor gave a banquet in honour of the Kent County Cricket Club and the Old Stagers whereat one of the founder members of 'O.S.' and 'I.Z.' gave a description of the very early days. Spencer Ponsonby-Fane, responding to the toast of Old Stagers, said:

'Fifty years is a long while to look back upon, and yet many of the incidents of our first journey here are still fresh in the memory. The trip down river in a steamer to Ramsgate, for there were no railways then, and the somewhat discomforting experience of some of us rounding the North Foreland in a lively breeze. The journey by coach to Canterbury — a very slow coach too — with plenty of glasses of ale at every village we passed through and our admiration and wonder at the first view of the beautiful City and Cathedral. This was followed by a hearty welcome by old Sam Wright at the Fountain Hotel with his never failing remedy for every contingency: "Never mind — let's have a bottle of Champagne". We were all, or nearly all, cricketers in those days and while we 'fretted our brief hour' on the stage by night we took part in the cricket by day. I well remember that on occasions we were kept down here, in town, cramming our parts into our heads and rehearsing for the evening performances, while our hearts were up on the cricket ground, with Pilch and Wenman — Felix and Mynn, and other cricket worthies of the day. Then there was the Old Theatre in Orange Street where our early performances took place. That is no pleasant reminiscence, for a more unsavoury den of dirt and distemper never existed. But we survived'.

Fifty years was indeed a very long time to look back upon, and another 100 years have passed since those words were delivered. As the Old Stagers turn the pages of their records, which contain every play-bill since 1842, copies of the epilogues, portraits, caricatures, press cuttings and photographs, the whole history of those 150 years of English life is reflected.

The unique feature of the Canterbury Week theatricals is the epilogue which ends the final performance on the last evening.

Begun as a tag, spoken by one of the leading actors or actresses, or maybe more than one, in the character which they had just presented, it developed into an entire scene which continued after the play had ended. Gradually the scene became more topical, wider in scope than the events of Cricket Week and reflecting upon the affairs of the day, social and political, in short a revue. The epilogue is characterised by its happy-go-lucky performance, its attempts to make its irreverence towards everything except cricket and Canterbury.

The script is never given to the performers until the beginning of the week and is learned, and rehearsed, entirely during the week. For many years now the Epilogue has ended with the appearance of the three spirits of the 'Week', ladies bearing banners representing 'The Spirit of Kent' — 'The Spirit of I. Zingari' — and 'The Spirit of Old Stagers', with their attendant supporters. Still, as in 1842, the Spirit of 'O.S.' asks the indulgence of the audience and bids them farewell until next year.

We can only hope that 50 years hence, the spirit of 'O.S.' will advance to the footlights and welcome the audience to its bi-centenary year. She might do worse than say as was said in 1842:
> "For the indulgence that our faults has spared,
> The sympathetic mirth our mirth that shared,
> The kindly laugh that left its echo here,
>   (hand placed on heart)
> We thank you, with gratitude sincere.
> Health, and long life, and happy hearts to all
> whose smiles have cheered and graced our festival."

CHAPTER 4

The Supporting Clubs

Three of the founders of I.Z. and O.S.: the Rt. Hon. Sir Spencer Ponsonby Fane,
Mr. John Loraine Baldwin and the Earl of Bessborough.

I. Zingari

ABOUT 145 years ago a few Cambridge undergraduates, among them F. Ponsonby and W. P. Bolland, were very interested in both cricket and acting. In 1845 William Bolland and a few of his friends played in a cricket match at Harrow and when they returned to London, J. L. Baldwin, who had driven them to Harrow, invited three of the cricketers — Frederick and Spencer Ponsonby-Fane and R. F. Long — to dinner at the Blenheim Hotel in Bond Street. During the course of the after dinner discussion a suggestion was made that a club should be formed "for the purpose of playing cricket and acting". They agreed "it should be a wandering club with no ground of its own" and that "members should promote the popularity of cricket far and wide".

The talk then turned to a name for the club. It is said that R. P. Long, who was fond of his claret and port, stirred from a comatose state murmured 'The Zingari of course', and promptly went to sleep. With eagerness his companions accepted the title of 'I. Zingari' (The Gypsies).

The next step was to frame a set of rules, some serious, some not so serious, many of which have survived to the present. They appointed W. P. Bolland Perpetual President and J. L. Baldwin Annual Vice President, positions which both hold to this day, and twenty of their friends as members. In addition to the Perpetual President and Annual Vice President, there were Treasurer and Auditor — The Hon. Robert Grimston, Liberal Legal Adviser — T. Taylor and Secretary — R. P. Long and these officers, with a biennial committee of six, ran the club in its early days.

They adopted as their colours Black, Red and Gold but how this originates is shrouded in mystery. In their book 'The History of I. Zingari' (Stanley Paul & Co Ltd, 1982) R. L. Arrowsmith and B. J. W. Hill give three versions. In 1845 a dinner was held for which C. G. Taylor presented colours to the club which were White with a narrow, Pale Blue stripe, spaced at intervals of about one inch. These colours were so similar to those of Cambridge that they were replaced, it is thought, by R. P. Long who was at that time Secretary of I.Z. A sketch dated 20th June 1846 shows a member wearing a broad brimmed hat with the crown decorated with the present colours of I.Z. and since that date the colours appear constantly in the records of the club.

However, R. P. Long subsequently tells the story that while travelling to Spain with two Cambridge friends, they encountered a gypsy girl who, after having her palms crossed with silver, told their fortunes. The story continues that, having taken a fancy to a scarf she was wearing, they bought it from her. She explained to them that the colours of Black, Red and Gold had a special meaning "Out of Darkness – through fire – into light". There is a slightly different version of the same story which was related by relatives of Long. According to them, Long was on his honeymoon in Spain and he and his wife visited a gypsy encampment. They were very much impressed by the performance of a particular dancer. When the dance ended Long requested permission to cross her palm with silver, as is customary. The girl agreed but said the custom of her tribe was never to accept gifts without giving something in return. All she had was a scarf that covered her head which she gave to Long explaining that the colours, Black, Red and Gold, symbolised the history of her tribe 'I. Zingari' (The Wanderers) who had escaped from slavery (Black) through blood (Red) to a land of promise (Gold). However, as we are told in the History of I.Z., as Long did not marry until 1853, this incident, if it did occur, cannot refer to the origins of I.Z. colours although it gained some credence with the family.

Mr. Arrowsmith and Mr. Hill gave a third version which was contained in a speech made by Sir Spencer Ponsonby-Fane after an I.Z. dinner in 1904. In it he explained that an original member of I.Z., Tom Taylor, visited Croatia in search of material for a book, and brought back some handkerchiefs coloured Black, Red and Gold. These colours were adopted by I.Z. as corresponding somewhat akin to the aims and ideals of the club. Whatever the true story may be, it seems unlikely it will ever be discovered.

Still on the question of colours, it is perhaps a little known fact that they are worn by the Old Stagers during Canterbury Week to mark the close association of these two bodies although the Old Stagers, as we have learned from a previous chapter, are about three years senior to I.Z. What then, is the connection between them? It stems from the Amateur Dramatic Society formed by friends at Cambridge who were interested in both acting and cricket and who began by staging theatricals during the first Canterbury Week in 1842. Most of the old Stagers were also cricketers, indeed thirteen of the original members of I.Z. were Old

Stagers, so it could be true to say that Canterbury Cricket Week and the O.S. gave birth to I.Z. The first occasion on which an I.Z. eleven took the field in a Canterbury Week was in 1848, when Kent v England finished early on Wednesday afternoon. Accounts have it that, 'there being a good company on the ground', eleven of I.Z. challenged the best eleven County Gentlemen and made a showy game for two hours. Again, in 1849, the Kent England match finished on Tuesday and the ever present and prepared I.Z. went to the wickets to contend against eight Gentlemen and three invited professionals, I.Z. winning the match by 34 runs.

These were of course early days in the life of Canterbury Week, I.Z. and O.S. Later, when the Kent County Cricket Club was rising to eminence and Canterbury Cricket Week was being regarded as one of the most important and happiest of cricket festivals, I.Z. cricket disappeared from the Canterbury scene but acting, which was the second of the club's original objects, flourished and to this day the tradition of their founders is still upheld most worthily by the Old Stagers.

Any celebration is a great occasion, albeit it is merely a milestone in the path of progress. It would, perhaps, be fitting to recall the achievements of the past bearing in mind they are the foundations on which the future is built. The years that followed the first world war (1914-1918) meant making a choice between closing down altogether or trying to rebuild the fortunes of the club on the old lines but under new conditions. Despite many difficulties, the officers chose the latter and soon a complete recovery was made. Following the second world war (1939-1945) the situation was again fraught with difficulties. So many young cricketers who, in the years before would have been glad to play, found it impossible, for many and varied reasons, to find the time. All credit then is due to the officers of the club for keeping the club alive.

Although I.Z. cricket disappeared from Canterbury Cricket Week many years ago, the club has played an important role in building the history of the 'Week' and maintaining its traditions throughout the years. It can claim, too, a contribution to the fortunes of the Kent County Cricket Club since it was reorganised on its present basis in 1870. An unbroken succession of members of I.Z. can be found in the records of Kent C.C.C. from its very early days, and from the year 1869 a number of members have held the important office of President of the County Club. It is also true to say that the County Committee has seldom, if ever, been without at least one member of I.Z. Among such names we find Frank Marchant, W. H. Patterson, Stanley Christopherson and Lord Harris who were trustees, whilst G. de L. Hough and Col. L. H. W. Troughton were secretaries of the club. With this in mind I.Z. can, with some confidence, claim that Kent County Cricket owes a small part of its success to their wise counsel. They may also claim that the example of the many members who, from time to time, have been members of the County Eleven contributed to the character and spirit of cricket and its popularity.

Although, as has been said, I.Z. cricket is no longer played in the 'Week', they nowadays share the Band of Brothers tent. Together they have survived two world wars and many modern changes. Long may their happy association continue for the enjoyment of all connected with the great institutions that make up the Canterbury Cricket Week.

Let us close this chapter with the message of the 1928 version of the 'Spirit' of I.Z.:

There's a motto of our order every cricketer should know,
And whatever fate or fortune has in store,
It will help you in your wanderings as through the world you
  go,
If you always keep this motto to the fore.
When luck seems all against you and everything looks blue,
And there's nothing left to do but stick it,
You must always keep your temper, you must keep your
  promise too
And throughout the game of life keep up your wicket.

The Band of Brothers

This famous amateur club whose flag of Black and Kentish Grey is a familiar sight on the St Lawrence ground, The Mote and other Kent grounds during annual cricket weeks, was one of the earliest of those 'wandering clubs' with no ground of their own, and the senior of all those identified with a single county. It began, as did so many English institutions, without any deliberate intention of developing in any particular way. Born as a small association of young men of East Kent with a common interest in cricket, it at once acquired a Kentish flavour, for the convenience of Canterbury

Week as a meeting place bound the new club with the cricket of the 'Week'. In the formative years of the 'Week' and up to the early 1860s, the principal matches in the 'Week', as we have already learned, were usually Kent v England and Gentlemen of Kent v Gentlemen of England or M.C.C. It was quite a regular thing that if one of these matches finished early the members of the B.B. and I.Z. clubs would put on a match for the benefit of spectators.

This early connection between the County's cricket and the cricket of B.B. became a firm alliance when the Fourth Lord Harris became captain of the Kent XI in 1875. It was about this time, when the County's cricket was at a dismal low, that Lord Harris set out on the one hand to build the professional strength of the County Club and on the other to direct, for the benefit of Kent cricket, the amateur strength of the County through the Band of Brothers. The reward of Lord Harris's policy came nine years after the founding of the Tonbridge Nursery, with the winning of the County Championship four times in eight years – 1906/1913. Every member of B.B. recognises to this day that membership implies the pleasure and duty to give whatever support he can to cricket in general and Kent cricket in particular. They were the first 'wandering club' to acquire a definite allegiance to a County and their action has been imitated, with some success, by the formation of such County amateur clubs as the Yorkshire Gentlemen, the Hampshire Hogs, the Devon Dumplings, the Sussex Martlets and others. But it is doubtful if any has quite the strong association with the County Club as B.B. and Kent. The continuing aim of the Band of Brothers is to play cricket keenly but cheerfully, as all should do, and, almost of equal importance, to play their part in the furtherance of Kent cricket in whatever way may seem to be the best in the changing times of modern life.

CHAPTER 5

The St. Lawrence Ground

N O story of Canterbury and Cricket Week would be complete
unless it included a chapter on the ground which has a history
of its own. Originally it formed part of the possessions of the
hospital of St Lawrence which was founded in 1137 for leprous
monks and the poor parents and relatives of the monks of
St Augustine. It was also said to have been at some time part of the
pleasure grounds of St Lawrence house, the seat of the Rookes, an
ancient Kentish family. However, when in 1847 the ground was first
used to host Cricket Week it was part of Winters Farm, Nackington,
from whom it was rented until it was purchased by the club from
Lord Sondes in 1896.

Harry Bass – Head groundsman 1879 - 1903.

Harry Bass leading the horse pulling a harrow covered with twigs which acted as a brush – 1900. (photo courtesy Brian Fitch)

Changes were of course inevitable both for the accommodation of the players and spectators. The print of the Jubilee Week in 1891 shows no permanent building on the ground except for a thatched wooden shed standing by the screen in a position where the pavilion now stands. This was later removed on rollers to a corner of the ground before being finally demolished in the late 1930s to make way for the secretary's office.

In 1892 a white shed and telegraph office was erected to the south of the pavilion. The scorers and press occupied the top half whilst the bottom was used as a storage space for nets and tools. Both this and a small wooden enclosure were pulled down in 1926 to make way for the concrete stand for many years now known as the Frank Woolley Stand.

The first real attempt to provide covered seating for spectators came in 1897 with the building of the iron stand at the Nackington

The assistant groundsman guides the horse drawn roller. The pavilion is nearing completion – 1900.
(Note the protective pads on the hooves of the horse)
(Photo courtesy of Brian Fitch)

Road end. It was for a long time referred to as the Ladies Stand. A scoreboard was added to the top a few years before the outbreak of the first world war in 1914. There then followed the building of the pavilion in 1900 and the annexe in 1909. Around 1928 a small white scoreboard was erected south of the concrete stand but, after only one season, it was moved to its present site next to the annexe. This scoreboard was presented by Major G. E. Meakin in memory of Frank Penn, a great Kent batsman. The last building to be built was the New Stand which was opened in 1985 by the club's patron, H.R.H. The Duke of Kent.

Before the erection of these buildings the arrangements for the players were much the same as when the ground was first used in 1847. They changed in a small tent and had no lunch provided except perhaps once a year when they were entertained by the mayor or on those occasions when Lord Harris invited them to his tent. Other than these occasions the amateurs relied on friends who either had tents or lived near the ground. The professionals had to provide for themselves around the ground or at the Bat and Ball. It was not until the late 1890s that a lunch tent was provided for the two teams and with the building of the pavilion came proper changing rooms and a dining room.

Although no new buildings were put up between 1926 and 1985 a number of alterations were made to existing buildings. At the end

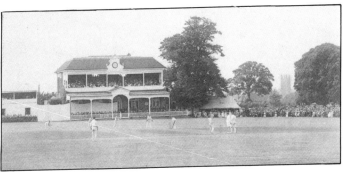

(a)

(b)

The pavilion as it appeared (a) in 1906 and (b) 1910. The annexe on the right was added in 1909. The telegraph stand and enclosure to the left were demolished in 1925 to make way for the new concrete stand.

of the 1969 season the pavilion was gutted and refurbished without altering the original outside structure. At the same time the tea kiosk which stood in the space between the pavilion and the annexe was demolished to make room for the new kitchen and players' dressing rooms. It was reopened in 1970 by the club's president Lord Harris and renamed The Stuart Chiesman pavilion in honour of a past chairman and great benefactor of the club. It was around this time too that the iron stand was converted into sixteen private hospitality boxes, again without any change to the original exterior, and reopened as the Leslie Ames Stand. The concrete stand has not undergone any major alteration except for the change of name. Thus, two great players and servants of Kent cricket have been honoured.

Gradually the long serving wooden benches which provide the free seating area and other seating in enclosures and stands, have been replaced by more modern seating. All these alterations have been carried out with care and have in no way detracted from the character of the ground.

A view of the ground in 1906 showing in the background the iron stand erected in 1897. It is now been named the Leslie Ames stand and converted into hospitality boxes. The framework is the original structure.

The St. Lawrence ground during the 2nd Test trial – England v The Rest – 1946.

The wickets at St Lawrence ground have always been noted for their trueness. This, in the first instance, was due to the care and devotion of Fuller Pilch who was first charged with the laying out of the ground, and his successors. In the history of the ground there have only been eight groundsmen. When Fuller Pilch retired in 1869 he was replaced by – Ladd, who in turn was succeeded by Harry Bass. Bass was to remain for twenty-five years and for a very short time the ground was in the care of – Fagg. Joe Murrin was next to be appointed and he remained in charge until his untimely death in 1946, within a few days of the date set for his retirement. Joe was a splendid judge of the game and a trusted friend and adviser to generations of players. In 1927 the county club committee paid him a great compliment in their report. Among the many arguments in favour of moving the nursery from Tonbridge to Canterbury they said it would be a distinct advantage to have the young players under his disciplinary supervision. During the war years 1940/1945 he managed to provide good wickets for anywhere up to 150 matches a year, despite being crippled by lameness. He had, during all this time, trained up a very good assistant in Jack Knell who, in turn, retired in 1962 after 41 years with the club, the last sixteen as head groundsman. Ted Baker was the next man in charge, and he was succeeded in 1970 by the present groundsman Brian Fitch.

County cricket was of course, suspended during the periods of the two world wars 1914/1918 and 1939/1945. During these times the St Lawrence ground was under military occupation. It was, however, kept open for minor cricket in which at least one of the

H.R.H. The Duke of Kent — patron — opens the new stand during the 1986 'Week'. He is accompanied by the president — Fraser Bird — and the chairman — Major M. A. O'B ffrench-Blake.

H.R.H. The Duke of Kent shares a smile and a joke with head groundsman Brian Fitch and his assistant Sam Fidler. Canterbury Week 1986.

sides would have been drawn from the armed services. During the 1914/1918 war nothing more than this was attempted and no effort was made to mark what would have been, in normal times, the 'Week'. However, from 1939 until 1945 on August Bank holiday each year a match of some public interest was arranged. No gate was charged but a collection would be taken for charity. These matches were for the most part well attended and something of the spirit of the 'Week' preserved by the Mayor of Canterbury Alderman C. Lefevre who entertained both teams to lunch.

In the first world war the ground did not suffer any damage from enemy action but in the second a large number of incendiary bombs fell on the roof of the concrete stand. A few did fall on the playing area but, except to a motor mower, did little damage.

1. RESULTS OF ALL FIRST-CLASS AND 'IMPORTANT' MATCHES

In the early years, when one of the principal matches finished before the schedule time, and there was sufficient time available, a scratch match would hastily be arranged to fill out time. These matches, although played in the 'Week' are not included below but will be found appended.

Year	Team	Score	Opponent	Score	Result
1842	Kent	278 & 44	England	266 & 58/1	Eng
	Gnts Kent	185 & 254	Gnts England	112 & 154	Gnts Kt
1843	Kent	152 & 24/1	England	82 & 93	Kt
	Gnts Kent	162 & 47	Gnts England	94 & 84	Gnts Kt
1844	Kent	94 & 37	England	96 & 87	Eng
	Gnts Kent	107 & 64	Gnts England	119 & 25/6	Drawn
1845	Kent	109 & 87	England	65 & 162	Eng
	Gnts Kent	205 & 80/1	Gnts Eng	188	Drawn
1846	Kent	94	England	49 & 42	Kt
	Gnts Kent	91 & 137	Gnts England	152 & 172	Gnts Eng
1847	Kent	172 & 53/7	England	67 & 154	Kt
	Gnts Kent	96 & 99	Gnts England	108 & 88/3	Gnts Eng
1848	Kent	125 & 5/0	England	83 & 46	Kt
	Gnts Kent	41 & 79	Gnts England	143	Gnts Eng
1849	Kent	127 & 227	England	48 & 100	Kt
	Gnts Kent	123 & 95	Gnts England	89 & 145	Gnts Eng
1850	Kent	94 & 163	England	156 & 116	Eng
	Gnts Kent	95 & 165/9	Gnts England	153 & 106	Gnts Kt
1851	Kent	105 & 115	England	162 & 59/6	Eng
	Gnts Kent	287 & 252/5	Gnts England	238	Drawn
1852	Kent	112 & 52	England	166	Eng
	Gnts Kent	116 & 90	Gnts England	142 & 156	Gnts Eng
1853	Kent	47 & 98	England	324	Eng
	Gnts Kent	107 & 119	Gnts England	209 & 20/3	Gnts Eng
1854	Kent	166 & 143	England	231 & 81/3	Eng
	Gnts Kent	113 & 112	Gnts England	167 & 107	Gnts Eng
1855	Kent/Surrey	165 & 133	England	151 & 138	Kt/Sry
	Gnts Kent/Surrey	51 & 79	Gnt England	91 & 187	Gnts Eng
1856	Kent/Sussex	165 & 26/4	England	71 & 119	Kt/Ssx
	Gnts Kent/Sussex	184 & 109/7	Gnts England	99 & 192	Gnts Kt/Ssx
1857	Kent/Sussex	135 & 67	England	186 & 166	Eng
	Gnts Kent/Sussex	143 & 85	Gnts England	67 & 119	Gnts Kt/Ssx
1858	Kent	85 & 103	England	66 & 126/5	Eng
	Gnts Kent	214	Gnts England	94 & 42/1	Drawn
1859	Sth Thames	48 & 146	Nth Thames	107 & 167	Nth
	Gnts Kent	137 & 17/1	Gnts England	30 & 123	Gnts Kt
1860	16 Kent	152	England	64 & 40	Kt
	Gnts Kent	96 & 163	M.C.C.	92 & 124	Gnts Kt

Year	Team	Scores	Opponent	Scores	Result
1861	14 Kent	134 & 148	England	98 & 130	Kt
	Gnts Kent	111 & 103	M.C.C.	175 & 103	M.C.C.
1862	14 Kent	171 & 236	England	105 & 132	Kt
	Gnts Kent	141 & 99	M.C.C.	344	M.C.C.
1863	13 Kent	191 & 65	England	131 & 150	Eng
	Gnts Kent	87 & 207	M.C.C.	187 & 108/9	M.C.C.
1864	13 Kent	57 & 82	England	222	Eng
	Gnts Kent	135 & 114	M.C.C.	192 & 298	M.C.C.
1865	Sth Thames	148 & 141	Nth Thames	105 & 157	Sth
	Kent	103 & 86/7	M.C.C.	120 & 66	Kt
1866	Sth Thames	73 & 119	Nth Thames	46 & 148/8	Nth
	Gnts Kent	150 & 75/3	M.C.C.	85 & 139	Gnts Kt
1867	Sth Thames	122 & 72	Nth Thames	169 & 141	Nth
	Kent	76 & 105	M.C.C.	230	M.C.C.
1868	Sth Thames	284 & 196	Nth Thames	252 & 286	Nth
	Kent	145 & 148	M.C.C.	199 & 226	M.C.C.
1869	Sth Thames	83 & 179/2	Nth Thames	107 & 154	Sth
	Kent	203 & 158	M.C.C.	449	M.C.C.
1870	Sth Thames	220 & 240/6	Nth Thames	236 & 278	Drawn
	Gnts Kent	96 & 131	M.C.C.	145 & 84/1	M.C.C.
1871	Sth Thames	250 & 143	Nth Thames	203 & 90	Sth
	Kent	120 & 150	M.C.C.	317	M.C.C.
1872	Sth Thames	131 & 142	Nth Thames	319	Nth
	Kent	169 & 107	M.C.C.	204 & 73/6	M.C.C.
1873	Sth Thames	369 & 95/3	Nth Thames	270 & 192	Sth
	Kent	141 & 171	M.C.C.	206 & 107/2	M.C.C.
1874	Kent/Glouc	231 & 247	England	201 & 223	Kt/Glouc
	Kent	168 & 141	M.C.C.	362	M.C.C.
1875	Kent/Glouc	248 & 44/4	England	220 & 68	Kt/Glouc
	Kent	262 & 109/5	M.C.C.	103 & 267	Kt
1876	Kent/Glouc	345 & 206/8	England	226 & 355	Drawn
	Kent	473	M.C.C.	144 & 344	Drawn
1877	Kent	229 & 342	England	209 & 32/2	Drawn
	Kent	177 & 74	M.C.C.	178 & 74/1	M.C.C.
1878	13 Kent	294 & 73/4	England	192 & 174	Kt
	Kent	216 & 20/2	M.C.C.	109 & 126	Kt
1879	13 Kent	142 & 174	England	72 & 246/6	Eng
	Gnts Kent	181 & 87	Gnts England	241 & 158	Gnts Eng
1880	13 Kent	189 & 142/9	England	172 & 157	Kt
	Gnts Kent	155 & 209/5	Gnts England	163	Drawn
1881	13 Kent	94 & 157	England	224 & 28/0	Eng
	Kent	143 & 80/2	Gnts England	92 & 130	Kt
1882	Kent	222 & 165	Australians	307 & 81/3	Aust
	Kent	195 & 188	Middlesex	338 & 46/0	Middx
1883	Kent	164 & 194	M.C.C.	295 & 64/1	M.C.C.
	Kent	216 & 118	Middlesex	294 & 41/1	Mddx
1884	Kent	169 & 212	Australians	177 & 109	Kt
	Kent	169 & 209	Middlesex	206 & 173/5	Middx
1885	Kent	312	Yorkshire	138 & 99/4	Drawn
	Kent	257	M.C.C.	99 & 119	Kt

Year	Team	Kent Score	Opponent	Opponent Score	Result
1886	Kent	171 & 35/0	Australians	79 & 123	Kt
	Kent	335 & 64/4	Yorkshire	172 & 226	Kt
1887	Kent	129 & 227/6	Yorkshire	559	Drawn
	Kent	241 & 364	Middlesex	412	Drawn
1888	Kent	107 & 80	Australians	116 & 152	Aust
	Kent	210 & 23/1	Lancashire	96 & 65	Kt
1889	Kent	256	Middlesex	90 & 111	Kt
	Kent	353 & 71/4	Gloucestershire	217 & 214	Drawn
1890	Kent	145 & 205	Australians	114 & 128	Kt
	Kent	177 & 228	Surrey	215 & 149/9	Drawn
1891	Kent	94 & 38/1	Gloucestershire	101 & 110/5	Drawn
	Kent	69 & 104	Surrey	169 & 7/0	Sry
1892	Kent	256 & 253	Gloucestershire	91 & 118	Kt
	Kent	164 & 184	Nottinghamshire	226 & 178	Notts
1893	Kent	127 & 198	Australians	229 & 60	Kt
	Kent	202 & 259/8	Nottinghamshire	336 & 1/1	Drawn
1894	Kent	171 & 187/5	Warwickshire	122	Drawn
	Kent	123 & 115	Yorkshire	213 & 26/0	Yorks
1895	Kent	278	Warwickshire	144 & 119	Kt
	Kent	135 & 139	Yorkshire	224 & 51/3	Yorks
1896	Kent	385	Lancashire	237 & 293/6	Drawn
	Kent	196 & 141	Australians	310 & 203	Aust
1897	Kent	199 & 181	Lancashire	399	Lancs
	Kent	170 & 202	Yorkshire	366 & 8/0	Yorks
1898	Kent	275 & 172/2	Lancashire	252 & 324/4	Drawn
	Kent	270 & 98/3	Nottinghamshire	345 & 171/7	Drawn
1899	Kent	305 & 209/4	Lancashire	197 & 190/6	Drawn
	Kent	184 & 141/8	Australians	227 & 94	Kt
1900	Kent	139 & 279	Lancashire	158 & 82/8	Drawn
	Kent	169/8 & 62/1	Surrey	171	Drawn
1901	Kent	311 & 177/3	Essex	432 & 176/8	Drawn
	Kent	293 & 202/6	Surrey	171	Drawn
1902	Kent	273 & 63/3	Essex	331	Drawn
	Kent	389	Surrey	139 & 59	Kt
1903	Kent	324 & 47/0	Essex	121 & 248	Kt
	Kent	172 & 354/5	Worcestershire	254 & 70	Kt
1904	Kent	392 & 253	Essex	332 & 94	Kt
	Kent	435 & 107/4	Surrey	216 & 321	Kt
1905	Kent	246 & 176	Essex	187 & 163/8	Drawn
	Kent	162 & 348	Lancashire	479 & 34/2	Lancs
1906	Kent	568	Sussex	170 & 261	Kt
	Kent	479	Lancashire	169 & 115	Kt
1907	Kent	353 & 112/3	Sussex	210 & 436/3	Drawn
	Kent	300 & 139	Lancashire	236 & 290	Lancs
1908	Kent	360	Sussex	173 & 177	Kt
	Kent	203 & 240	Hampshire	178 & 268/9	Hants
1909	Kent	278	Middlesex	78 & 163	Kt
	Kent	406 & 30/0	Hampshire	236 & 199	Kt
1910	Kent	412	Middlesex	96 & 166	Kt
	Kent	291	Gloucestershire	55 & 140	Kt

Year	Team	Score	Opponent	Score	Result
1911	Kent	324 & 223/3	Hampshire	399 & 319	Drawn
	Kent	156 & 294	Lancashire	429 & 24/1	Lancs
1912	Kent	275	Hampshire	39/2	Drawn
	Kent	236	Nottinghamshire	58 & 58	Kt
1913	Kent	215 & 359	Sussex	212 & 122	Kt
	Kent	294	Nottinghamshire	308 & 28/5	Drawn
1914	Kent	291 & 137	Sussex	384 & 78/8	Ssx
	Kent	301	Northampton- shire	70 & 179	Kt
1919	Kent	339	Essex	494 & 65/2	Drawn
	Kent	301 & 172/5	Aust Imp Forces	198 & 419/8	Drawn
1920	Kent	163 & 255	Hampshire	99 & 154	Kt
	Kent	217 & 117	Middlesex	212 & 127	Mddx
1921	Kent	316/9 & 107/2	Hampshire	68 & 351	Kt
	Kent	280 & 274	Middlesex	137 & 174	Kt
1922	Kent	166 & 90/1	Hampshire	224 & 248	Drawn
	Kent	276	Middlesex	124 & 122	Kt
1923	Kent	480/9	Hampshire	123 & 300	Kt
	Kent	445 & 159	Middlesex	457 & 148/3	Mddx
1924	Kent	330/9	Hampshire	172 & 137	Kt
	Kent	67 & 229	Nottinghamshire	242 & 55/0	Notts
1925	Kent	232 & 100/4	Hampshire	170 & 161	Kt
	Kent	349/8	Sussex	196 & 136	Kt
1926	Kent	412 & 172/1	Hampshire	144 & 439	Kt
	Kent	413	Essex	267 & 123	Kt
1927	Kent	407	Hampshire	81 & 234	Kt
	Kent	370	Nottinghamshire	116 & 131	Kt
1928	Kent	309/7	Somerset	100 & 195	Kt
	Kent	346 & 226/1	Essex	208 & 218	Kt
1929	Kent	339	Gloucestershire	217 & 137/1	Drawn
	Kent	186 & 58/5	Nottinghamshire	155 & 125	Drawn
1930	Kent	271	Hampshire	98	Drawn
	Kent	279 & 182/8	Nottinghamshire	248 & 91/5	Drawn
1931	Kent	145 & 48/2	Somerset	122 & 67	Kt
	Kent	299	Derbyshire	125 & 209/7	Drawn
1932	Kent	163 & 197	Gloucestershire	325 & 38/1	Glouc
	Kent	376	Glamorgan	118 & 89	Kt
1933	Kent	389 & 85/0	Hampshire	344 & 357/9	Drawn
	Kent	209 & 229	Derbyshire	84 & 194	Kt
1934	Kent	392	Somerset	272 & 106	Kt
	Kent	445/6	Nottinghamshire	116 & 175	Kt
1935	Kent	335 & 135	Gloucestershire	316 & 94	Kt
	Kent	333 & 226/7	Nottinghamshire	433	Drawn
1936	Kent	108 & 148/4	Hampshire	125 & 217/8	Drawn
	Kent	275 & 197/7	Lancashire	232 & 241/5	Lancs
1937	Kent	273 & 311	Hampshire	203 & 243	Kt
	Kent	332 & 242/9	Nottinghamshire	265 & 311/5	Notts
1938	Kent	407	Hampshire	102 & 197	Kt
	Kent	329 & 205	Lancashire	246 & 163	Kt

Year	Team	Kent score	Opponent	Opponent score	Result
1939	Kent	161 & 83	Hampshire	135 & 111/3	Hants
	Kent	138 & 156	Middlesex	358	Mddx
1946	Kent	477	Hampshire	299 & 173	Kt
	Kent	126 & 139	Somerset	328	Som
1947	Kent	445/7	Hampshire	285 & 116	Kt
	Kent	423/8 & 181/6	Middlesex	225 & 429/8	Drawn
1948	Kent	390/9	Hampshire	163 & 228/5	Drawn
	Kent	390/8 & 169	Nottinghamshire	326 & 78/4	Drawn
1949	Kent	413/8	Hampshire	203 & 183	Kt
	Kent	211 & 293	Middlesex	362/7 & 249/3	Middx
1950	Kent	235 & 102/1	Hampshire	81 & 358/6	Drawn
	Kent	254/6 & 239/6	Middlesex	249 & 241/3	Kt
1951	Kent	263	Hampshire	122/5	Drawn
	Kent	190 & 144	Middlesex	208/5 & 243/8	Mddx
1952	Kent	150/4 & 175/9	Hampshire	138 & 216/3	Drawn
	Kent	179 & 272	Derbyshire	340 & 107/8	Drawn
1953	Kent	219 & 197/8	Hampshire	210 & 228	Drawn
	Kent	129 & 163	Middlesex	216/9 & 175/6	Mddx
1954	Kent	220 & 212	Hampshire	172 & 182/6	Drawn
	Kent	325/7	Middlesex	318/7	Drawn
1955	Kent	217 & 222	Hampshire	309/8 & 160/9	Hants
	Kent	360/9	Gloucestershire	144 & 308/4	
1956	Kent	126 & 142/9	Hampshire	132 & 139/6	Drawn
	Kent	296 & 121/4	Lancashire	258 & 156	Kt
1957	Kent	257 & 197/9	Hampshire	186 & 194	Kt
	Kent	310/6	Essex	144 & 182/4	Drawn
1958	Kent	172 & 285	Hampshire	378/7 & 82/6	Hants
	Kent	208	Derbyshire	100 & 100	Kt
1959	Kent	80 & 267	Hampshire	280 & 69/2	Hants
	Kent	232 & 117	Derbyshire	257 & 191	Derby
1960	Kent	251 & 50/1	Hampshire	134 & 292/9	Drawn
	Kent	183 & 266/8	Derbyshire	116 & 143	Kt
1961	Kent	369	Hampshire	300/6 & 165	Drawn
	Kent	233 & 222	Gloucestershire	309 & 170	Glouc
1962	Kent	326/9	Hampshire	16/0	Drawn
	Kent	182 & 205/5	Glamorgan	245/6 & 139/5	Kt
1963	Kent	77 & 387/6	Hampshire	235 & 181/8	Drawn
	Kent	475/6	Leicestershire	222 & 159	Kt
1964	Kent	388/5 & 177/6	Hampshire	322/9 & 224/8	Drawn
	Kent	246 & 236/8	Middlesex	252 & 240/6	Drawn

1965	Kent	106 & 141/7	Hampshire	121 & 154/6	Drawn
	Kent	138 & 269/9	Middlesex	73 & 258	Kt
1966	Kent	128/7 & 89/5	Leicestershire	88 & 63	Kt
	Kent	99 & 312	Warwickshire	250	Drawn
1967	Kent	187	Leicestershire	280 & 135/9	Drawn
	Kent	223 & 100	Yorkshire	225 & 99/3	Yorks
1968	Kent	299 & 47/0	Warwickshire	173 & 172	Kt
	Kent	81 & 136/5	Yorkshire	93 & 2/0	Drawn
1969	Kent	254 & 137	Gloucestershire	176 & 92/7	Drawn
	Kent	208 & 263/7	Leicestershire	354/7	Drawn
1970	Kent	172 & 218/6	Worcestershire	309/8 & 147/3	Drawn
	Kent	207 & 243/4	Middlesex	95 & 319/7	Drawn
1971	Kent	416/4	Middlesex	354/6	Drawn
	Kent	250	Yorkshire	90 & 131	Kt
1972	Kent	302/7 & 181/3	Glamorgan	318/4 & 164	Kt
	Kent	372/5 & 65/1	Sussex	243 & 193	Kt
1973	Kent	316/7	Sussex	123 & 16/2	Drawn
	Kent	330/8 & 195/5	Yorkshire	268 & 145/3	Drawn
1974	Kent	89 & 146	Middlesex	298/6	Mddx
	Kent	296	Warwickshire	146 & 243/4	Drawn
1975	Kent	306/8 & 83/7	Hampshire	385/6 & 278/9	Drawn
	Kent	179 & 275	Middlesex	430/4 & 180/3	Drawn
1976	Kent	251 & 369	Gloucestershire	374/7 & 250/3	Glouc
	Kent	307/8 & 203/6	Surrey	334/7 & 242/4	Drawn
1977	Kent	148 & 51	Worcestershire	125/9 & 75/4	Worc
	Kent	307/6 & 38/2	Nottinghamshire	129 & 212	Kt
1978	Kent	338/8 & 157/5	Leicestershire	255/6 & 120	Kt
	Kent	195 & 122/3	Warwickshire	120 & 64/4	Drawn
1979	Kent	160 & 386/5	Worcestershire	286 & 30/2	Drawn
	Kent	345/2 & 170/3	Yorkshire	224 & 14/2	Drawn
1980	Kent	301/7 & 206/6	Glamorgan	266 & 242/7	Glam
	Kent	325/7 & 241/6	Warwickshire	228 & 175	Kt
1981	Kent	166 & 126	Essex	310 & 126/6	Essex
	Kent	315 & 205/7	Hampshire	217 & 122	Kt
1982	Kent	209 & 284/8	Essex	248 & 261/4	Drawn
	Kent	300/8 & 164/5	Glamorgan	368/7 & 235/3	Drawn
1983	Kent	276 & 199/7	Worcestershire	376 & 141	Drawn
	Kent	343/8 & 121/7	Surrey	233 & 235/6	Sry

Year	Kent	Score	Opponent	Opponent Score	Result
1984	Kent	235 & 126/3	Leicestershire	197	Drawn
	Kent	236 & 246/8	Surrey	183 & 124	Kt
1985	Kent	171 & 290	Sussex	317 & 27/0	Ssx
	Kent	164 & 4/0	Warwickshire	300/7 & 138/6	Drawn
1986	Kent	329/8 & 87	Leicestershire	199 & 212	Kt
	Kent	431/8	Hampshire	234 & 181/5	Drawn
1987	Kent	212 & 192/3	Derbyshire	318	Drawn
	Kent	176 & 185/9	Middlesex	291 & 103/6	Drawn
1988	Kent	121 & 185	Somerset	452/4	Som
	Kent	327 & 140/6	Leicestershire	247 & 203/7	Drawn
1989	Kent	287 & 141	Warwickshire	250/8 & 181/0	Wwk
	Kent	346 & 184/2	Surrey	302 & 230/3	Sry
1990	Kent	449/2 & 140	Middlesex	308/3 & 276/8	Drawn
	Kent	250/8 & 194/8	Worcestershire	351/7 & 170/5	Drawn
1991	Kent	358 & 103/7	Surrey	178 & 385	Drawn
	Kent	290 & 203/5	Hampshire	241 & 196/7	Drawn

SUMMARY OF RESULTS OF ALL FIRST-CLASS AND 'IMPORTANT' MATCHES

Match				Drawn	
Kent v England	24	Kent	10	England	13	Drawn	1
Gnts Kent v Gnts Eng	17	Gnts Kent	4	Gnts Eng	8	"	5
Kt/Sry v Eng	1	Kt/Sry	1	Eng	0	"	0
Gnts Kt/Sry v Gnts Eng	1	Gnts Kt/Sry	0	Gnts Eng	1	"	0
Kt/Ssx v Eng	2	Kt/Ssx	1	Eng	1	"	0
Gnts Kt/Ssx v Gnts Eng	2	Gnts Kt/Ssx	2	Gnts Eng	0	"	0
S. Thames v N. Thames	10	S. Thames	4	N. Thames	5	"	1
Gnts Kent v M.C.C.	7	Gnts Kt	2	M.C.C.	5	"	0
Kent v M.C.C.	14	Kent	4	M.C.C.	9	"	1
Kt/Glouc v Eng	3	Kt/Glouc	2	Eng	0	"	1
Kent v Gnts Eng	1	Kent	1	Gnts Eng	0	"	0
Kent v Australians	8	Kent	5	Australians	3	"	0
Kent v A.I.F.	1	Kent	0	A.I.F.	0	"	1
Kent v Derbyshire	7	Kent	3	Derbyshire	1	"	3
Kent v Essex	11	Kent	4	Essex	1	"	6
Kent v Glamorgan	5	Kent	3	Glamorgan	1	"	1
Kent v Gloucestershire	11	Kent	3	Gloucestershire	3	"	5
Kent v Hampshire	42	Kent	15	Hampshire	5	"	22
Kent v Lancashire	13	Kent	4	Lancashire	5	"	4
Kent v Leicestershire	8	Kent	4	Leicestershire	0	"	4
Kent v Middlesex	26	Kent	7	Middlesex	10	"	9
Kent v Northamptonshire	1	Kent	1	Northamptonshire	0	"	0
Kent v Nottinghamshire	14	Kent	4	Nottinghamshire	3	"	7
Kent v Somerset	5	Kent	3	Somerset	2	"	0
Kent v Surrey	11	Kent	3	Surrey	3	"	5

Kent v Sussex	9 Kent	5 Sussex	2	"	2
Kent v Warwickshire	9 Kent	3 Warwickshire	1	"	5
Kent v Worcestershire	6 Kent	1 Worcestershire	1	"	4
Kent v Yorkshire	11 Kent	2 Yorkshire	4	"	5
TOTAL 280		101	87	"	92

OTHER MATCHES

1846	Gents	60	Players	53	Gnts
1848	Gnts Kent	120	I. Zingari	62/4	Drawn
1849	I. Zingari	87	8 Gnts 3 Players	53	I.Z.
1851	Gnts E. Kent	44	I. Zingari	204	I.Z.
1852	Gnts Kt	dnb	I. Zingari	111	Drawn
1853	Kent	76	I. Zingari	108	I.Z.
	Scratch XI	165	Scratch XI	74/5	Drawn
1857	Gnts Kent	111	I. Zingari	76/5	Drawn
1858	Gnts Kent	86	I. Zingari	99 & 81/9	Drawn
1859	Gnts Kent	152	I. Zingari	54/6	Drawn
1860	Band of Brothers	79	I. Zingari	80/5	I.Z.
	Gnts Kent	dnb	I. Zingari	56/2	Drawn
1861	Band of Brothers	119	I. Zingari	200	I.Z.
1862	Band of Brothers	124/8	I. Zingari	122	B.B.
1863	Band of Brothers	115	I. Zingari	284	I.Z.
1864	Kent Garrisons	151 & 144	I. Zingari	137 & 118	Garri
1865	Kent Garrisons	70 & 47/3	I. Zingari	324	Drawn
1866	Gnts Sth	97 & 226	I. Zingari	78 & 124	Gnts
1867	Gnts Kent	109 & 332	I. Zingari	99	Drawn
1868	Kent	160	I. Zingari	147/5	Drawn
1869	Gnts Kent	345	I. Zingari	dnb	Drawn
1870	Gnts Kent	256/5	I. Zingari	242	Kt
1871	Gnts Kent	104	I. Zingari	158 & 183/9	Drawn
1872	Gnts Kent	163	I. Zingari	151 & 128/4	Drawn
1873	Gnts Kent	114	I. Zingari	253	I.Z.
1874	Gnts Kent	163 & 74	I. Zingari	172 & 66/4	I.Z.
1875	Gnts Kent	152/8	I. Zingari	214	Drawn
1877	Gnts Kent	76/6	Gnts Eng	308	Drawn

2. HUNDREDS SCORED

In the 280 matches played between 1842 and 1991, 196 individual hundreds have been recorded, the highest being 344 by W. G. Grace for M.C.C. v Kent in 1876. W. G. Grace was also the first player to score a hundred in each innings of a match in the 'Week': (130 & 102* for South Thames v North Thames) in 1868. Since that date the feat has been accomplished on six other occasions:

W. G. GRACE whose record innings of 344, made in 1876, remains to this day the highest individual score on the St Lawrence ground. He was also the first player to score a hundred in each innings of a match in the 'Week'.

C. B. Fry	123 & 112	
D. B. Carr	150* & 109	
D. A. Livingstone	117 & 105*	
N. G. Featherstone	127* & 100*	
Zaheer Abbas	230* & 104*	
M. R. Ramprakash	100* & 125	

	for Hampshire	1911
	" Derbyshire	1959
	" Hampshire	1964
	" Middlesex	1975
	" Gloucestershire	1976
	" Middlesex	1990

1853	J. Ceasar	
1856	Hon. S. Ponsonby	
1862	E. M. Grace	
1868	W. G. Grace	
	W. G. Grace	
	Rev J. M'Cormick	
1869	W. G. Grace	
1871	W. G. Grace	
1872	R. A. Mitchell	
1874	W. G. Grace	
	W. G. Grace	
1875	F. Penn	
1876	W. R. Gilbert	
	A. J. Webbe	
	W. G. Grace	
	Lord Harris	
1877	F. Penn	
1800	Hon. A. Lyttleton	
1882	E. F. S. Tylecote	
	Lord Harris	
1883	C. T. Studd	
1886	G. G. Hearne	
	C. Wilson	
1887	L. Hall	
	G. Ullyett	
	F. Lee	
	F. Hearne	
	A. J. Webbe	
1889	L. Wilson	
	O. G. Radcliffe	
1890	L. A. H. Hamilton	
1892	A. Hearne	
	A. Shrewsbury	
1893	A. Shrewsbury	
	Rev. W. Rashleigh	
1894	Rev. W. Rashleigh	
1895	J. R. Mason	
1896	J. R. Mason	
	Rev. W. Rashleigh	
	A. C. MacLaren	
	C. J. Burnup	
1897	A. C. MacLaren	
1898	J. T. Tyldesley	
	J. A. Dixon	

101	Eng v Kt
108	Gnts Eng v Gnts Kt/Ssx
192*	M.C.C. v Kt
130	Sth Thames v Nrth Thames
102*	Sth Thames v Nrth Thames
137	Nrth Thames v Sth Thames
127	M.C.C. v Kt
117	M.C.C. v Kt
125*	M.C.C. v Kt
121	Kt/Glouc v Eng
123	M.C.C. v Kt
101	Kt v M.C.C.
143	Kt/Glouc v Eng
109	Eng v Kt/Glouc
344	M.C.C. v Kt
154	Kt v M.C.C.
135	Kt v Eng
120	Gnts Eng v Gnts Kt
100*	Kt v Australians
101	Kt v Middlesex
105*	Middx v Kt
117	Kt v Yorks
127	Kt v Yorks
110	Yorks v Kt
124	Yorks v Kt
119	Yorks v Kt
144	Kt v Yorks
192	Mddx v Kt
132	Kt v Glouc
101	Glouc v Kt
117*	Kt v Aust
116*	Kt v Glouc
111*	Notts v Kt
124	Notts v Kt
101*	Kt v Notts
106	Kt v Warwick
100	Kt v Warwick
115	Kt v Lancs
109	Kt v Lancs
226*	Lancs v Kt
101	Kt v Aust
244	Lancs v Kt
127	Lancs v Kt
165	Notts v Kt

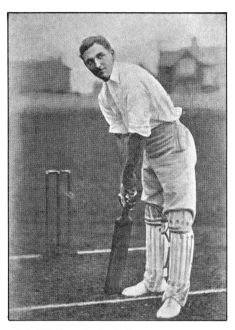

*C. B. FRY (Hampshire) only the second player, behind
W. G. Grace, to score a hundred | in each innings of a match.*

1901	E. W. Dillon	103*	Kt v Essex
	P. Perrin	104	Essex v Kt
1903	C. J. Burnup	129	Kt v Worcs
1904	J. R. Mason	133	Kt v Essex
	E. Humphries	104	Kt v Sry
	J. Seymour	105	Kt v Sry
	T. Hayward	188*	Sry v Kt
1905	J. Sharp	142	Lancs v Kt
1906	C. J. Burnup	141	Kt v Ssx
	R. N. R. Blaker	122	Kt v Ssx
	C. H. B. Marsham	119	Kt v Ssx
	K. L. Hutchings	176	Kt v Lancs
1907	J. R. Mason	121*	Kt v Ssx
	J. Vine	108	Ssx v Kt
	R. R. Relf	210	Ssx v Kt
	R. H. Spooner	134	Lancs v Kt
1908	S. H. Day	114	Kt v Ssx

FRANK WOOLLEY, holder of the highest individual score by a Kent player in matches of the 'Week'. 270 v Middlesex 1923.

1910	J. Seymour	193	Kt v Mddx
1911	F. E. Woolley	108	Kt v Hants
	K. L. Hutchings	103*	Kt v Hants
	C. B. Fry	123	Hants v Kt
	C. B. Fry	112	Hants v Kt
	J. Seymour	116*	Kt v Lancs
1914	J. Vine	140	Ssx v Kt
1919	H. T. W. Hardinge	172*	Kt v Essex
	A. C. Russell	160	Essex v Kt
1921	G. J. Bryan	179	Kt v Hants
	H. S. Altham	141	Hants v Kt
1922	C. P. Mead	100*	Hants v Kt
1923	J. L. Bryan	236	Kt v Hants
	F. E. Woolley	270	Kt v Middx
1924	F. E. Woolley	101	Kt v Hants
	W. W. Whysall	109*	Notts v Kt
1925	F. E. Woolley	118	Kt v Ssx
1926	H. T. W. Hardinge	117	Kt v Hants

*LES AMES, the batsman, became the second Kent player
and twelfth in the history of the game to score a hundred hundreds
when he made a match winning 131 v Middlesex in 1950.*

1926	A. P. F. Chapman	130	Kt v Hants
	C. P. Mead	175*	Hants v Kt
	J. P. Parker	156	Hants v Kt
	H. T. W. Hardinge	176	Kt v Essex
1927	J. L. Bryan	134	Kt v Notts
	C. P. Mead	128	Hants v Kt
1929	F. E. Woolley	119	Kt v Glouc
1930	W. W. Whysall	128	Notts v Kt
1932	L. E. G. Ames	130	Kt v Glam
	W. R. Hammond	136	Glouc v Kt
1933	W. H. Ashdown	106	Kt v Hants
	C. P. Mead	135	Hants v Kt
	F. E. Woolley	161	Kt v Derby
1934	F. E. Woolley	101	Kt v Notts
1935	L. J. Todd	128*	Kt v Glouc
	W. R. Hammond	163	Glouc v Kt

1936	B. H. Valentine	102*	Kt v Lancs
	J. Iddon	132	Lancs v Kt
1937	W. H. Ashdown	116	Kt v Hants
	B. H. Valentine	104	Kt v Hants
	L. J. Todd	135	Kt v Notts
	J. Hardstaff	126	Notts v Kt
1938	C. H. Knott	112	Kt v Hants
	A. E. Fagg	134	Kt v Lancs
1939	C. I. J. Smith	101*	Middx v Kt
1946	L. J. Todd	122	Kt v Hants
	B. H. Valentine	110	Kt v Hants
	J. D. Robinson	140	Middx v Kt
1947	A. E. Fagg	123	Kt v Hants
	J. E. Manners	121	Hants v Kt
	A. E. Fagg	184	Kt v Middx
	D. S. C. Compton	106	Mddx v Kt
	W. J. Edrich	130	Middx v Kt
1948	W. W. Keeton	109	Notts v Kt
1949	L. J. Todd	129	Kt v Middx
	S. M. Brown	200	Middx v Kt
1950	C. Walker	122	Hants v Kt
	H. A. Pawson	103	Kt v Middx
	L. E. G. Ames	131	Kt v Middx
1954	R. C. Wilson	131	Kt v Middx
1955	W. H. Rogers	103*	Hants v Kt
	D. M. Young	137	Glouc v Kt
	J. M. Allen	105	Kt v Glouc
1956	M. C. Cowdrey	121*	Kt v Lancs
1958	R. C. Wilson	127	Kt v Hants
	S. E. Leary	101	Kt v Derby
1959	M. C. Cowdrey	111	Kt v Hants
	D. B. Carr	156*	Derby v Kt
	D. B. Carr	109	Derby v Kt
1961	M. C. Cowdrey	156	Kt v Hants
	R. E. Marshall	131	Hants v Kt
1962	J. Presdee	130*	Glam v Kt
1963	P. E. Richardson	172	Kt v Hants
	S. E. Leary	132	Kt v Hants
	R. E. Marshall	119	Hants v Kt
1964	P. E. Richardson	124	Kt v Hants
	R. C. Wilson	130	Kt v Hants
	M. C. Cowdrey	100	Kt v Hants
	D. A. Livingstone	117	Hants v Kt
	D. A. Livingstone	105*	Hants v Kt
	M. C. Cowdrey	101	Kt v Middx
1965	B. W. Luckhurst	113	Kt v Middx
	W. E. Russell	114	Middx v Kt
1968	M. H. Denness	138	Kt v Warwick
1969	B. Duddleseton	171	Leic v Kt
1970	T. W. Graveney	114	Worcs v Kt

1971	B. W. Luckhurst	155*	Kt v Middx
	Asif Iqbal	103*	Kt v Middx
1972	M. H. Denness	162	Kt v Glam
	A. Jones	152*	Glam v Kt
1974	G. W. Johnson	158	Kt v Warwick
	A. I. Kallicharan	116*	Warwick v Kt
	M. J. Smith	170*	Middx v Kt
1975	J. N. Shepherd	116	Kt v Mddx
	M. J. Smith	107	Middx v Kt
	N. G. Featherstone	127*	Middx v Kt
	N. G. Featherstone	100*	Middx v Kt
1976	Zaheer Abbas	230*	Glouc v Kt
	Zaheer Abbas	104*	Glouc v Kt
	J. H. Edrich	114*	Sry v Kt
1977	C. J. Tavare	124*	Kt v Notts
	B. Hassan	106	Notts v Kt
1978	R. A. Woolmer	137	Kt v Leic
	Asif Iqbal	104*	Kt v Leic
	B. F. Davison	106	Leic v Kt
1979	C. J. Tavare	112	Kt v Worcs
	A. G. E. Ealham	153	Kt v Worcs
	Younis Ahmed	170	Worcs v Kt
1980	C. J. Tavare	100*	Kt v Glam
1981	K. S. McEwan	102	Essex v Kt
1982	G. A. Gooch	149	Essex v Kt
	A. Jones	136*	Glam v Kt
	D. A. Francis	142*	Glam v Kt
1983	R. A. Woolmer	120	Kt v Sry
1984	C. J. Tavare	117	Kt v Leic
	C. S. Cowdrey	102	Kt v Sry
	M. R. Benson	120	Kt v Sry
1985	A. I. Kallicharan	108	Warwk v Kt
1986	S. G. Hinks	131	Kt v Hants
	P. A. J. DeFreitas	106	Leic v Kt
	P. Willey	104	Leic v Kt
1987	B. Roberts	128	Derby v Kt
1988	R. F. Peinaar	128	Kt v Som
	S. R. Waugh	161	Som v Kt
	R. J. Bartlett	102*	Som v Kt
1989	N. R. Taylor	118	Kt v Sry
	S. G. Hinks	104*	Kt v Sry
	T. A. Lloyd	109	Warwk v Kt
1990	S. G. Hinks	234	Kt v Middx
	N. R. Taylor	152	Kt v Middx
	M. R. Ramprakash	100*	Middx v Kt
	M. W. Gatting	101	Middx v Kt
	M. R. Ramprakash	125	Middx v Kt
	P. A. Neale	119*	Worcs v Kt
1991	M. R. Benson	142	Kt v Sry
	M. V. Fleming	113	Kt v Sry
	D. J. Bicknell	151	Sry v Kt

SIMON HINKS (234) and NEIL TAYLOR (152) after their record second wicket partnership of 366 v Middlesex 1990.

3. TEN OR MORE WICKETS IN A MATCH

69 bowlers have performed this feat on 122 occasions in matches of the 'Week'. The most successful being A. P. Freeman (9), E. Willsher (8), C. Blythe (7), and W. G. Grace (6). However, only two bowlers have taken 10 wickets in an innings – E. M. Grace (10/69 for M.C.C. v Kent in 1862) and Jas Lillywhite Jnr (10/129 for Sth Thames v Nrth Thames in 1872).

Between the years 1842 and 1856 bowling analysis were not always kept, often the entry showed only total number of balls bowled against runs conceded for the innings. Similarly, a bowler would not always be credited with a wicket if the batsman was caught or stumped, only the catcher or stumpers name would be recorded. In the following where it is known that a bowler took ten or more wickets in a match these are shown without cost in runs.

1844	A. Mynn	6/121	& 6/42	Kt v Eng
	W. Clarke	6/30	& 6/26	Eng v Kt
1845	W. R. Hillyer	6/	& 4/	Kt v Eng
	W. Clarke	5/	& 7/	Eng v Kt
1846	W. R. Hillyer	7/28	& 4/15	Kt v Eng
1847	W. R. Hillyer	7/	& 4/	Kt v Eng
1848	A. Mynn	6/	& 5/	Kt v Eng
1849	J. Wisden	7/	& 5/	Eng v Kt
	E. Hinkly	8/	& 3/	Kt v Eng
1851	J. Grundy	8/	& 2/	Eng v Kt
1852	J. Grundy	3/48	& 7/26	Eng v Kt
1855	E. T. Drake	6/20	& 5/52	Gnts Eng v Gnts Kt
1856	E. Willsher	5/	& 5/	Kt/Ssx v Eng
1857	E. Willsher	4/55	& 6/46	Kt/Ssx v Eng
	J. B. Parker	5/26	& 5/41	Gnts Eng v Gnts Kt
1858	J. Grundy	4/32	& 7/42	Eng v Kt
	J. Jackson	9/35	& 4/55	Kt v Eng
1859	J. Jackson	7/21	& 5/53	N. Thames v S. Thames
1860	E. Willsher	8/16	& 3/14	16 Kt v Eng
	R. H. B. Marsham	7/50	& 3/5	M.C.C. v Gnts Kt
1861	E. Willsher	8/27	& 4/52	14 Kt v Eng
	H. Arkwright	9/43	& 9/53	M.C.C. v Gnts Kt
1862	E. M. Grace	5/77	& 10/69	M.C.C. v Kt
1863	T. Sewell Jnr	8/45	& 4/46	13 Kt v Eng
	G. A. Millman	5/45	& 7/65	M.C.C. v Gnts Kt
1864	G. Wootton	8/15	& 5/33	Eng v 13 Kt
	H. Arkwright	9/79	& 5/80	M.C.C. v Gnts Kt
1865	G. Bennett	4/35	& 8/61	S. Thames v N. Thames
1866	E. Willsher	7/24	& 3/47	S. Thames v N. Thames
1867	E. Willsher	4/45	& 6/57	S. Thames v N. Thames
	G. Wootton	7/78	& 5/42	N. Thames v S. Thames
1868	E. Willsher	4/51	& 6/46	Kt v M.C.C.

E. M. GRACE one of only two bowlers to take ten wickets in an innings in matches of the 'Week'.

1869	J. Southerton	4/61	& 6/74	S. Thames v N. Thames
1870	F. C. Cobden	6/36	& 6/83	M.C.C. v Kt
1871	E. Willsher	4/45	& 7/46	S. Thames v N. Thames
	W. M. Rose	4/9	& 8/71	N. Thames v S. Thames
	W. G. Grace	7/67	& 5/77	M.C.C. v Kt
1872	Jas Lillywhite jnr	10/129		S. Thames v N. Thames
	W. N. Powys	4/79	& 6/68	M.C.C. v Kt
1873	Jas Lillywhite jnr	8/114	& 6/58	S. Thames v N. Thames
	W. G. Grace	5/55	& 10/92	M.C.C. v Kt
1874	W. G. Grace	6/92	& 4/68	Kt/Glouc v Eng
	W. G. Grace	5/82	& 6/47	M.C.C. v Kt
1875	W. G. Grace	5/82	& 6/35	Kt/Glouc v Eng
1876	A. Shaw	5/78	& 5/61	Eng v Kt/Glouc
1878	A. Penn	5/43	& 5/48	Kt v M.C.C.
	W. Foord Kelcey	5/32	& 6/52	Kt v M.C.C.
1880	F. Morley	6/97	& 4/83	Eng v 13 Kt
	W. G. Grace	7/71	& 3/76	Gnts Kt v Gnts Eng

A. P. 'Tich' FREEMAN who took ten or more wickets in a match nine times between 1926 and 1935.

LES AMES, the wicket-keeper. ct or stmpd Ames b Freeman was a common entry in the scorebooks.

1935	T. W. J. Goddard	5/102	& 5/49	Glouc v Kt
	A. P. Freeman	6/116	& 4/22	Kt v Glouc
1938	L. L. Wilkinson	5/72	& 7/53	Lancs v Kt
1939	A. E. G. Baring	5/67	& 5/43	Hants v Kt
1947	D. V. P. Wright	5/123	& 5/35	Kt v Hants
1948	P. F. Harvey	3/113	& 7/55	Notts v Kt
1949	D. V. P. Wright	5/81	& 6/89	Kt v Hants
	J. A. Young	7/47	& 6/72	Middx v Kt
1951	J. A. Young	4/67	& 6/47	Middx v Kt
1952	C. Gladwin	4/36	& 6/81	Derby v Kt
1953	J. A. Young	6/55	& 8/60	Middx v Kt
1959	G. W. Richardson	3/68	& 7/31	Derby v Kt
1965	R. M. H. Cotton	6/38	& 4/36	Hants v Kt
1966	A. L. Dixon	5/25	& 5/33	Kt v Leic
1968	A. G. Nicholson	8/22	& 2/33	Yorks v Kt
	G. S. Sobers	7/69	& 4/87	Notts v Kt

1881	F. Morley	5/33	& 6/55	Eng v 13 Kt
	W. Foord Kelcey	5/47	& 6/65	Kt v Gnts Eng
1882	T. W. Garrett	6/62	& 6/58	Aust v Kt
1883	C. T. Studd	6/79	& 4/45	Middx v Kt
1884	G. E. Palmer	4/52	& 7/74	Aust v Kt
1885	J. Wootton	6/45	& 5/45	Kt v M.C.C.
1886	J. Wootton	5/40	& 5/60	Kt v Aust
	A. Hearne	6/61	& 4/80	Kt v Yorks
1888	C. T. B. Turner	4/41	& 6/28	Aust v Kt
1889	C. Wright	7/42	& 6/64	Kt v Middx
1890	C. T. B. Turner	5/55	& 5/53	Aust v Kt
1891	G. A. Lohman	6/14	& 4/28	Sry v Kt
1892	W. Hearne	3/64	& 7/75	Kt v Notts
	F. J. Shacklock	7/69	& 3/63	Notts v Kt
1895	F. S. Jackson	5/28	& 7/63	Yorks v Kt
1897	J. Briggs	6/55	& 7/80	Lancs v Kt
	F. S. Jackson	7/78	& 4/44	Yorks v Kt
1899	C. McLeod	7/87	& 3/41	Aust v Kt
1900	C. Blythe	6/40	& 5/32	Kt v Lancs
1901	W. M. Bradley	7/55	& 5/87	Kt v Sry
1903	C. Blythe	9/67	& 2/74	Kt v Essex
	A. Fielder	4/86	& 7/45	Kt v Worcs
1904	W. Reeves	4/144	& 6/83	Essex v Kt
1905	C. Blythe	4/88	& 6/62	Kt v Essex
	W. Brearley	6/81	& 5/122	Lancs v Kt
1906	A. Fielder		& 7/49	Kt v Lancs
1907	A. Fielder	9/108	& 4/65	Kt v Lancs
	L. W. Cook	7/105	& 4/75	Lancs v Kt
1908	C. B. Llewellyn	5/68	& 5/74	Hants v Kt
	C. Blythe	8/83	& 4/113	Kt v Hants
1910	C. Blythe	6/23	& 5/51	Kt v Glouc
1912	C. Blythe	5/28	& 6/28	Kt v Notts
1913	A. Fielder	7/41	& 3/38	Kt v Ssx
1914	C. Blythe	6/107	& 4/39	Kt v Ssx
	F. E. Woolley	5/23	& 5/65	Kt v N'Hants
1920	A. S. Kennedy	6/57	& 7/68	Hants v Kt
	F. E. Woolley	6/35	& 5/64	Kt v Hants
1922	F. E. Woolley	7/34	& 6/45	Kt v Middx
1924	C. S. Marriott	5/66	& 5/44	Kt v Hants
	F. C. Matthews	8/33	& 2/39	Notts v Kt
1925	C. S. Marriott	6/60	& 5/56	Kt v Hants
1926	A. P. Freeman	6/92	& 6/89	Kt v Essex
1927	A. P. Freeman	6/28	& 8/91	Kt v Hants
	A. P. Freeman	6/57	& 5/34	Kt v Notts
1928	A. P. Freeman	8/94	& 6/87	Kt v Essex
1929	A. P. Freeman	8/74	& 6/57	Kt v Notts
1930	A. P. Freeman	7/59	& 8/35	Kt v Som
1932	A. P. Freeman	7/42	& 6/42	Kt v Glam
1933	A. P. Freeman	6/30	& 6/82	Kt v Derby
1934	C. S. Marriott	4/27	& 7/56	Kt v Notts

(a)   (b)

(a) DEREK UNDERWOOD and (b) DOUG WRIGHT, two great Kent bowlers who also took ten or more wickets in a match.

1971	D. L. Underwood	5/19	& 5/41	Kt v Yorks
1972	R. A. Woolmer	6/70	& 7/65	Kt v Ssx
1974	P. H. Edmunds	7/38	& 4/53	Middx v Kt
1981	D. L. Underwood	7/93	& 5/61	Kt v Essex
	D. L. Ackfield	8/55	& 3/58	Essex v Kt
1983	D. L. Underwood	7/103	& 7/55	Kt v Yorks
1986	T. M. Alderman	8/70	& 6/74	Kt v Leic